Cake Eater

GETTING HIGH, HITTING LOW:
And Trying To Stay In The Middle

CARL RADKE

Cover Layout and Design © Nat Mack
Cover Photography: Daniel Rahal
Cover Hair: Jesus Peral [Marie Robinson Salon], Haley Wilkinson [Marie Robinson Salon]
Cover Makeup: Nikki Siminson
Cover Lighting: Dereck Brewer
Cover Studio: East of Normal [The Foreigner]
Cover Wardrobe: MR PORTER

Distributed by Simon & Schuster
Line Edit by Tina Beier

ISBN: 978-1-998076-76-5
Ebook: 978-1-998076-61-1

BIO005000   BIOGRAPHY & AUTOBIOGRAPHY / Entertainment & Performing Arts
BIO026000   BIOGRAPHY & AUTOBIOGRAPHY / Memoirs

#CakeEater

For my family, who lived through the darkest years with me and never walked away. You held me together when I was falling apart, and you're the reason I'm still here to tell this story.

For the fans, who saw my worst moments on TV and still chose to support my journey. Your messages, your encouragement, and your own stories of struggle and recovery reminded me that none of us are alone in this.

This memoir is the author's story. The memories and experiences are from his recollection and may not reflect the experiences of those featured in the book.

Cake Eater

Introduction

SOBER CARL'S NOT FUN.

Imagine not only hearing your friends say this about you but also having the rest of the world see the proof on TV.

There's an unspoken understanding that when we're not drinking, we're not fun. It's societal pressure to be "on" continuously, and alcohol is often the only way for many of us to be the star of the party.

This was my reality. In my first season on *Summer House*, I came down with tonsillitis after attending a wedding. The following weekend, I had to be on camera in the Hamptons, trying to be the fun, outgoing guy I usually am, but without drinking. The insecurities I usually kept pushed down started filling my mind until it was overwhelming. It was the same every time I tried to party sober. That feeling never really changed—I was there but not entirely in it.

None of us is born with an endless supply of ego and self-confidence. That's one of the reasons I spent so much time getting lost in alcohol and cocaine. If I wasn't drinking, did that mean everyone was going to hate me? Were the friendships I had worked so hard to build about to disappear? Did I not fit in anymore?

Starting my recovery journey felt like steering a boat through unfamiliar waters. The biggest issue wasn't craving a drink. It was dealing with the fear that people would think I had suddenly become boring. In my world, and most places, drinking was the thing that made any hangout feel electric. Without it, I felt like I was the only person who didn't get the joke, as if the energy had moved on without me.

It's a little embarrassing to admit, but until 2021, all I wanted was for people to think I was cool. That was how I measured my worth: by how I looked to people I didn't even know. We like to think we outgrow that, but most of us are still chasing it, whether we admit it or not.

The society also tends to equate sobriety with being dull. That's just not true.

Looking back at my twenties and early thirties, so much of my drinking was about the buzz and the vibe. It wasn't really about who I was with or what we were talking about. Sure, I was out with friends, laughing, clinking glasses, having a good time. But if you asked me to remember a deep conversation from those nights, I'd draw a blank. It's not that the nights didn't matter. It's that real connection was rare. We thought we were bonding, but we were just drinking together. So many of those late-night talks were about big dreams, like starting record labels or launching alcohol brands. We were chasing the high in every way, but nothing ever stuck. It was a blurry ambition.

Eventually, that fun catches up with you. You start making bad decisions, acting out, hurting the people you care about, and hurting yourself, too. It's a harsh realization, but I'll get into more of that later.

We grew up watching shows like The O.C. that made partying look glamorous. However, the bigger influence, at least here in the United States, is how drinking is marketed to us. "Work hard, play hard." If you're a kid born in 1985, like me, you remember life before the internet. You had to call your friend's landline and hope their parents didn't answer. Drinking was part of the culture. It was what we did at house parties, in basements, wherever we could.

My upbringing mirrored my dad's in many ways. I attended the same schools in Pittsburgh that he and his siblings attended. Our family was close, especially during tough times, like when we had to stay with my grandparents for a while. I was raised not just by my parents but also by my uncles, aunts, and grandparents.

Drinking was just part of the family rhythm. Friday nights meant thirty packs of beer, football, and pizza. The men drank beer, and the women had wine or cocktails. My grandfather, a Korean War vet with an old-school corporate job, would pour himself a martini after work. If he had more than a couple, you kept your distance. That was his way of unwinding. It was the *Mad Men* model: a drink for lunch, a drink after work, and then another before bed. That was the dream.

I still remember the first time I drank. I was just a kid, and I grabbed my dad's Budweiser right out of his hand. That red can, that bitter taste; I can still picture it. Back then, it felt like a rite of passage. Now, I see it differently. We've started talking more about addiction and how alcohol messes with us in ways we don't even realize.

The thing is, alcohol still gets a pass. It's been wreaking havoc on lives forever, and we still build celebrations around it. It becomes an excuse, too. "Sorry, I was drunk" is a get-out-of-jail-free card for stuff we might've wanted to do anyway. Without booze, we'd have to admit we made those choices. That's a tough pill to swallow.

Looking back at being a teenager, it makes sense why alcohol became the go-to solution. Everything felt awkward. You were trying to figure out who you were into, how to talk to people, and how to just be. And fitting in? That was the whole game. Whether it was getting a seat at the cool kids' table, making the right team, or just surviving high school and college, alcohol felt like the secret password that got you through the door.

In my world, everything was a competition. Who was the smartest, the most athletic, and whose family had money? We had social rankings before social media even existed. And alcohol was always part of the picture. It was just there.

The idea that not drinking makes you boring really messes with your head. I used to joke that I was only interesting after a couple of whiskeys and something extra. But the truth is, underneath that joke was a real fear—that without the buzz, maybe I didn't have a personality at all. That kind of thinking builds a complex. You start to believe the only version of you people like is the one that's altered. And you begin to lose sight of who you are.

Now that I'm sober, "fun" means something else. It means being present. It means connection. Back in the day, fun meant staying up all night. Now, it means remembering every laugh, every conversation. That means more.

Anyone who has gone through a change like this knows what I'm talking about. The little things matter more. The right people matter more. It's not about what you're wearing or what you own. It's about who's showing up for you and how you show up for yourself. That's where the magic is. And recovery? That's what helps you find it.

Fun for me now is quieter. It's fewer people but stronger connections. I used to think I was having fun, but really, I was just playing a part. I was hurting. Now, the fun is real. It's me being me. And if that doesn't work for someone, that's okay.

I no longer need to be the center of attention. I can sit with a non-alcoholic beer, talk about the game, or catch up with someone I haven't seen in a while. And when I'm ready to go, I go. No pressure to stay. It's about quality now, not quantity. And time—that's the most valuable thing we have. I don't waste it anymore.

The shift from "Sober Carl is not fun" to just "Sober Carl" has been one of the most significant transformations of my life. I've had to unpack what happiness actually looks like. It's not found in a round of shots or a champagne toast. It's found in conversations I remember, relationships that matter, and a version of myself I finally recognize.

If you're questioning who you are without a drink, if you're scared of becoming boring or being left behind, I understand. But trust me, the real you is in there. And once you meet that person, you'll wonder why you ever needed anything else.

Recovery isn't the end of the fun. It's the start of something better. It's a genuine connection, absolute joy, and real life. The kind that doesn't fade by morning.

Chapter 1

I GREW UP IN a family where Pittsburgh roots ran deep and success was kind of expected. My parents had one of those all-American college love stories. They met at Yale, where my dad played football and my mom worked in the athletic department. After they graduated, they moved to Chicago to start their life together, and not long after, I showed up. I made my grand entrance in January 1985, weighing in at a solid ten pounds, six ounces. I've never been one to do anything small, even from day one.

Those early years in Chicago were marked by both warmth and uncertainty. We lived in a friendly Midwestern suburb with sidewalks where kids rode bikes and school buses picked up students. But beneath the surface, financial struggles were brewing. The stock market's volatility in the late 80s hit my father's career hard. By the time I was five or six, we faced foreclosure on our house and had to downsize to an apartment.

It was in that apartment where one of my most infamous childhood stories took place. At just three years old, I had already developed quite the appetite and a knack for breaking into any food storage my parents attempted to keep me out of. One day, while my mom was cleaning, I decided I wanted some gummy bears. Without a word to anyone, I set off on my own down a busy road, my feet clad only in socks, and walked a full mile to the nearest drugstore. I grabbed the gummy bears and started eating them right there in the aisle. A family friend happened to spot me, and before I knew it, I was being rushed back home to my panicked mom. Looking back, it's a funny story, but it hints at the impulsive streak and tendency to use food as comfort that would emerge later in my life. At the time, though, I was just a determined little kid doing whatever it took to get what I wanted.

In 1990, when I was five, we made the pivotal move back to Pittsburgh, back to my father's roots and the support of extended family. We moved in with my grandparents in Upper St. Clair, a community that would become the backdrop for much of my youth. My grandfather, the Korean War vet, he carried a quiet sense of discipline and pride that shaped how we did things at home. Sundays meant church, the lawn was always trimmed, and there was a big focus on working hard and doing well in school. That was just the rhythm of our life growing up.

But even as we settled into this idyllic-seeming suburban existence, the seeds of future turmoil were already taking root.

Once we got settled in Pittsburgh, it became pretty clear that our situation was different from most families around us. At first, we lived in my grandparents' finished basement, then eventually moved into an apartment complex just outside Upper St. Clair. It wasn't a terrible place by any means, but in a town full of big houses and perfectly cut lawns, we definitely stood out.

I started kindergarten while living with my grandparents, who dropped me off each morning as my parents worked full-time jobs. Later, when we moved to the apartment, I'd be ferried to and from school by my dad, never taking the bus like most of my classmates. It might not seem like a big deal, but things like that made it clear we didn't really fit the Upper St. Clair mold. That apartment complex became a reminder of the financial stress we were under, and I felt it even as a kid. When classmates invited me over after school, I always said yes, but I never returned the offer. I was too embarrassed for them to see how small our place was. I'd make excuses or say my parents weren't home, anything to avoid letting people in. It wasn't just about space. It was about not wanting anyone to see what our life actually looked like behind closed doors. Instead, I became the perpetual guest, always visiting others' homes but never hosting.

It wasn't until I was about seven that our situation improved somewhat. My parents ended up renting a little house in Upper St. Clair—it used to be where a coal miner lived back in the day. By Upper St. Clair standards, it wasn't much, but to me? It felt like we'd hit the jackpot. The place had character, I'll give it that. Curtis and I ended up sharing a room, which seemed totally normal at the time. But looking back, man, I had no idea how much being crammed in there together would end up mattering. When Curtis started going through his rough patch, I had a front-row seat to all of it.

In those early years, though, Curtis was everything I wanted to be. He was five years older than me and an incredible athlete who had this way about him that drew everyone in. The guy seemed like he could do anything. But as I entered my preteen years, the cracks in this idealized image began to show. Curtis started high school as I was in the middle of elementary, and the reports that filtered down to me were troubling. There were whispers of drinking, of fights, of trouble with the law.

One incident stands out vividly in my memory. It was either my eleventh or twelfth birthday, and I had two close friends over to watch football. We were upstairs when a knock came at the door. Looking out the window, we saw five police cars parked outside. Officers entered our home with a warrant, there to arrest Curtis for an incident at a convenience store the day before.

I'll never forget the sight of my brother handcuffed on the stairs, looking up at me and my friends as we were ushered past him. "I'm so sorry, guys," he said, his voice filled with shame. My dad had to call my friends' fathers to come pick them up early, explaining awkwardly that Curtis had "found himself in some trouble."

That whole thing really opened my eyes to what was happening with our family and how people saw us around town. The Radke name used to mean something good—sports, good grades, etcetera. But now, it was starting to mean something else entirely. I could feel that shift happening, and it hit me hard. I knew right then that I had to figure out who I was going to be, separate from all the drama that seemed to follow Curtis wherever he went.

As Curtis's struggles intensified, I threw myself into being the perfect son. I joined the student council, excelled in sports, and maintained top grades. I became an altar boy at our church, serving dutifully every Sunday. On the outside,

I had it all figured out—good grades, popular, doing all the right things. But on the inside, I was total chaos. I was pissed off, confused, and if I'm being honest, scared as hell that maybe I had whatever Curtis had in me, too. Like maybe it was just a matter of time before I screwed up everything just like he did.

Little did I know then that this fear and the coping mechanisms I was developing to deal with it would play a significant role in my own journey towards addiction and, eventually, recovery. But that part of the story was still years away. For now, I was just trying to get through being a teenager, which was hard enough on its own. But I also had to watch Curtis—my hero, my big brother—slowly disappear into a dark place that I couldn't even begin to wrap my head around.

As I entered high school, the contrast between my brother's path and mine became even more pronounced. While Curtis struggled to find his footing, I threw myself into every opportunity Upper St. Clair High School offered. I threw myself into everything—student council, sports, you name it. My grades became an obsession because I had my sights set on one thing: Syracuse University's Newhouse School. It was legendary for broadcast journalism, and I knew that's where I wanted to be.

This ambition wasn't only about career prospects. It was my ticket out, a chance to forge an identity separate from the family drama that had come to define so much of my adolescence. I'd spend hours watching ESPN, memorizing the catchphrases of anchors like Dan Patrick and Stuart Scott, dreaming of the day I'd be behind that desk myself.

One memory stands out from my freshman year. I came home from soccer practice one afternoon and, without a word to my mom, changed into a full suit and tie. When she asked where I was going, I casually replied, "I'm going to speak at the school board." It was part of my duties as a freshman student council member, but to me, it represented so much more. It was my shot to prove that not all Radkes were screw-ups—to show everyone, including myself, that our family name could mean something good again.

But no matter how hard I worked to keep everything looking perfect on the outside, things at home were falling apart. Curtis's addiction was getting worse, and our house had turned into a painful cycle—one day we'd think he was getting better, the next day everything would go to hell again. There were moments of promise, such as when Curtis turned things around in his senior year of high school, becoming a star baseball player and even hitting a home run at Three Rivers Stadium. But those good moments never lasted—we'd always come crashing back down.

College was basically the worst place Curtis could end up—all that partying and easy access to whatever he wanted. It was like sending him straight into a danger zone.

When Curtis left for school, I had mixed feelings. Part of me was honestly relieved—I could finally come home without wondering what kind of mess I'd be walking into. But then I'd feel terrible for thinking that way about my own brother. Even with him gone, his addiction was still a heavy weight on our whole family, no matter how far away he was.

Around that time, I started spending more and more time at my friends' houses. My best friend Matt's family became my second family. They gave me something I was desperate for: stability. They'd have me over for dinner, drive me to games, and their house became a safe place I could escape to when things got too heavy at home.

But even when I was hanging out with them, I felt like I didn't quite belong. The differences between my family and theirs were pretty obvious. They went on actual vacations, drove nice cars, and lived in a big house with multiple bathrooms. Meanwhile, we were still renting our tiny place with one bathroom for all of us. I was wearing hand-me-downs while my friends had all the latest stuff. To a teenager, those things feel huge.

What really got to me though, was how people saw me at school. I'd be walking through school and someone would go, "Wait, you're Curtis's brother?" And I could just see it—they were looking at me like I was some kind of ticking time bomb. Wondering if I was gonna screw up just like he did. That question followed me around everywhere.

It really started screwing with me. I kept thinking, *Am I gonna end up like Curtis?* Because that's what everyone says, right—addiction runs in families. So maybe it was just a matter of time. That fear became a voice in the back of my head, and looking back, I think it set me up for my own problems later on.

I was carrying way too much for a kid. Trying to be the perfect son, perfect student, perfect athlete, all while dealing with the shame and confusion of having an addict for a brother. I had no clue how to handle all these feelings, and our family wasn't exactly big on talking things through. The Radke way was to suck it up and keep moving.

As high school went on, the gap between how things looked on the outside and what I was feeling inside got bigger and bigger. On paper, everything was great: good grades, killing it in volleyball and other sports, student government, the whole thing. But underneath all that success, I was a mess waiting to happen.

My brother's stint in college had ended as many of us had feared it might. After nearly two years, he was kicked out. We never got the full story about what happened, but it was obvious that Curtis was in even worse shape than when he left. When he came back home, all the drama and unpredictability came right back with him.

I was a junior in high school when Curtis showed up again, and honestly, the timing sucked. As I prepared for college applications and the SATs, trying to keep my focus on my dream of attending Syracuse, our home life once again became a battleground.

The lack of privacy in our shared bedroom meant that I had a front-row seat to Curtis's downward spiral. I witnessed late-night phone calls, erratic behavior, and the physical toll that years of substance abuse had taken on my once-athletic brother. There were times when I'd wake up in the middle of the night to find him gone, only to have him stumble in as I was getting ready for school.

I doubled down on my efforts to maintain my image at school. I went completely overboard with my college applications. Syracuse University wasn't just where I wanted to go—it was my way out. My chance to be someone other than "Curtis's little brother" and all the baggage that came with it.

It was during this time that I began to develop coping mechanisms that would later prove destructive. I started thinking that if I could just be perfect at everything, somehow that would fix all the craziness at home. Like if I was good enough, achieved enough, maybe I could make it all better. That thinking really messed me up—I was setting these impossible standards for myself that I could never actually hit.

Senior year was this weird mix of everything I wanted and everything I was scared of. Getting into Syracuse was incredible—for the minute after receiving my acceptance letter, I forgot about the family drama and just felt pure happiness. But as graduation got closer, I started freaking out. What was going to happen when I left? Who was going to deal with Curtis and keep my parents sane? And honestly, I had no idea who I was going to be once I wasn't "the good Radke brother" anymore.

The summer before college was a blur of preparation and anticipation. But it was also marked by a growing restlessness. As my departure for Syracuse loomed, a part of me longed to rebel, to shed the perfectionist skin I had worn for so long.

Part of me was ready to go wild once I got away from everything. All that family stuff I'd been dealing with? I never really worked through any of it—I just buried it and tried to be perfect instead. That combination was going to bite me in the ass later, but I had no clue at the time.

When I was throwing my stuff into boxes for Syracuse, I was excited as hell but scared too. I genuinely believed that getting away from Pittsburgh was going to fix me. Like I could just drive far enough away, and suddenly I wouldn't be dealing with all the family crap anymore. Pretty stupid when I think about it now.

My first weeks at Syracuse were a whirlwind of new experiences. For the first time in my life, I wasn't "Curtis's brother" or "the Radke kid." I was just Carl, a freshman with a clean slate. The freedom was intoxicating, and I threw myself into college life with abandon.

But old habits die hard, and I soon found myself falling into familiar patterns. I joined clubs, signed up for challenging classes, and tried to be everything to everyone. On the surface, I was the picture of a successful college student. But the cracks were beginning to show.

It started innocently enough, a beer at a party here, a missed class there. But soon, I found myself drawn to the party scene in a way that scared me. Alcohol became a way to quiet the perfectionist voice in my head, to numb the anxieties that had followed me from Pittsburgh.

My first year at Syracuse, I started noticing things about myself that really freaked me out. I was acting like Curtis did when his problems first started. The exact thing I was terrified of happening was actually happening. But I couldn't admit that—not even to myself. That would mean I was a total failure. So I just shoved those thoughts way down and kept telling myself I was fine, that I had it all figured out.

Except this is a key indicator of denial. Not dealing with my problem head-on meant I was basically following the same path Curtis took. I was nowhere near getting clean—that was still years down the road, buried under all the drinking and all the crap I refused to deal with from my family.

But even when things were getting really bad, some tiny part of me still believed I could turn it around. The lessons of resilience I had learned from my family and the strength I had developed in the face of adversity would eventually become the foundation of my recovery. But first, I had to hit rock bottom to face the very demons I had spent so long running from.

Chapter 2

WHEN I GOT TO Syracuse in the fall of 2003, I was pumped but nervous as hell. Walking around campus and seeing the Newhouse School right there was an out-of-body experience. That was where I was going to become the next big sportscaster. All those years of dreaming about it, and I was here. This was my shot to create a new life for myself, away from all the family stuff back in Pittsburgh.

Getting into Syracuse hadn't been easy. My SAT scores had barely topped 1000, which was well below the 1200 most students achieved. But I was determined. Through perseverance, a lucky break, and some networking help from my uncle, I managed to land an interview. The morning of that interview is still so clear in my mind. I'd been at a homecoming party the night before and drinking way more than I should have. As my parents drove me to the hotel, I was fighting through a brutal hangover. Right before we got to the entrance, I couldn't hold it anymore and threw up in a planter outside. Somehow, that cleared my head enough to nail the interview. Looking back now, I can see that was an early warning sign about my relationship with alcohol that would follow me for years.

But getting accepted was just the beginning. The bigger challenge was figuring out how to pay for it. Syracuse was expensive—like $50,000 a year expensive. For a kid whose family had been renting the same house for $860 a month for as long as they could remember, this seemed an insurmountable amount of money. My parents sat me down for an honest talk about money, making it crystal clear that if this was what I wanted, I'd have to figure out how to make it happen myself.

That's when something surprising happened. My uncle spotted an ad in the *Pittsburgh Post-Gazette* for a scholarship from a wealthy local family. The requirements? You had to be from Pittsburgh and be a member of the Lutheran church. I checked both boxes. I poured everything into that essay, writing about growing up around addiction and mental health issues, about wanting more diversity and a broader perspective than what I had in Upper St. Clair.

I was in Ocean City with a buddy when my dad called. I could hear the emotion in his voice when he told me I'd won all four years of college paid for. At seventeen, I had no clue what a huge deal that was. It took me years to realize that moment basically changed my whole life.

So, there I was, only eighteen, stepping into a world that was exactly what I'd dreamed of but nothing I was prepared for. In the early 2000s, Syracuse was consistently ranked among the top party schools in America. That whole scene ended up screwing with my relationship with alcohol for the next ten years.

Syracuse's social stuff was way more intense than I thought it would be. There were so many different groups, and everyone was trying to figure out where they fit in. You had the Jewish kids who had known each other from summer camps since they were little, the Boston crew, the New York City socialites, and then everyone else. As a Pittsburgh kid, I was definitely in the "everyone else" category, constantly trying to find my place.

Syracuse was a melting pot of students from diverse backgrounds, many of whom came from affluent families in New York, New Jersey, and New England. I found myself surrounded by kids who never had to worry about money, who drove BMWs their parents had bought for them, and who treated their parents' credit cards as if they were unlimited. It was nothing like how I grew up in Pittsburgh, and I felt that difference every day.

To fit in, I started to reshape myself into what I thought was the "cool college guy." I got a job at Abercrombie & Fitch, partly for the employee discount and partly to hang out with hot coworkers. I grew out my hair into what we called "hockey hair." I started hitting the tanning beds regularly, trying to get that look that was the standard among the popular crowd.

But more than anything else, I drank. Alcohol became my great equalizer, the thing that could make a kid from Pittsburgh fit in with trust fund babies from Manhattan. It started innocently enough: a beer at a party, a shot with new friends. Before long, I was fully immersed in Syracuse's infamous party scene.

Joining a fraternity seemed like the perfect solution to my social anxiety. It offered instant brotherhood, a packed social calendar, and, most importantly, a place where I belonged. In my freshman year, I was introduced to the "dirty rush" pledging before the official rush period. Frat life appealed to me; it gave me that sense of belonging I was looking for. My dad had been in a fraternity at Yale, and I had this romanticized version of what that meant, fueled by movies like *Animal House* and *Van Wilder*.

The pledging process was a crash course in binge drinking. I recall one particularly brutal night during Hell Week. We were locked in the frat house basement for twenty-four hours straight, forced to stay awake and go through various "challenges." One involved a group of us finishing an entire handle of whiskey. To this day, the smell of whiskey makes me want to puke. I ended up stumbling back to my dorm, barely able to walk, thinking this was just what college was about.

It wasn't just the drinking. Being in a fraternity opened doors to a social world I had only glimpsed before. Suddenly, I was getting invited to the best parties, hanging with the "cool" crowd, and feeling like I was finally part of something. Of course, almost all these social interactions revolved around alcohol. It was our common language, the thing that broke down barriers and made everyone feel equal, regardless of where they came from or the wealth of their parents.

As I moved through college, my drinking got worse. By senior year, it wasn't unusual for me to show up to a party or tailgate with a thirty-pack of Natty Ice, fully planning on drinking most of it myself. We'd go to the grocery store and figure out ways to swipe beer, like hiding cases under the cart where the cashiers wouldn't see them. Looking back, it was pretty damn stupid, and we could've gotten in serious trouble. But man, the adrenaline rush when we pulled it off made us want to do it more.

Academically, I was determined to succeed. I busted my ass to get into New-house, so I wasn't about to blow it. No matter how destroyed I was from the night before, I dragged myself to every single class. It was a chaotic double life I was living. During the day, I'd be the perfect student—taking notes, asking questions, the whole thing. But come nighttime? I was the guy doing keg stands and downing shots like I had nothing to lose.

This Jekyll and Hyde dual life became my regular. I took pride in being able to party hard and still maintain my grades. I saw it as a badge of honor, proof that I could handle everything. What I didn't realize then was that I was creating a pattern that would follow me long after graduation, using alcohol as a crutch for social situations and stress management.

Sophomore year brought new experiences. Spring break in Acapulco was my first time trying cocaine. Despite the initial hesitation—after all, cocaine was what my brother did—I found myself drawn in by what it promised: more energy and more confidence. That first night, doing lines before hitting the club, felt electric. I remember thinking, "This is what I've been missing." It opened a door that would be hard to close later on.

Back on campus, drugs became more common in my circle. Adderall for all-nighters during finals, weed to chill after stress, and cocaine to keep partying. We told ourselves it was all just part of the college experience. Looking back now, I can see how we were using these substances to fill these empty spots inside us, to quiet our insecurities, to feel like we belonged.

My body image issues, which started back in high school, grew way worse during this time. I became obsessed with looking a certain way, convinced my appearance was the key to being accepted. There were times when I would binge eat while high, then purge because I felt guilty and terrified of gaining weight. It was a vicious cycle, fueled by booze and drugs and hidden behind what looked like typical college partying. Nobody questioned it because everyone was doing something in excess.

During my junior year, I moved off-campus with two older guys from the volleyball team. Living with them exposed me to an even more intense party lifestyle. They drank every single day, before class, after class, and sometimes even during class. It became completely normal to crack open a beer at any hour, to pregame before heading out, and to keep the party going until sunrise. My tolerance went through the roof, and what once would have been a wild night became just another Tuesday.

When Facebook launched during my sophomore year, it added another layer to the social dynamic. Suddenly, we could see information about everyone on campus. It became a tool for social climbing, for determining who belonged to which circle and how to gain invitations to the right parties. I'd be on there for hours, just scrolling through random people's profiles and friending anyone who might make me look better. We were playing the same old popularity game, except now it was on the computer, too.

Despite all the partying, I managed to maintain my academic performance. I was proud that I could balance everything: my social life, studying, and extracurricular activities. I was involved in the student council, played club volleyball, and even worked as a PA announcer for women's volleyball games. From the outside, I probably looked like I had everything figured out.

Underneath, things were starting to crack. The drinking that began as a way to fit in had become something I relied on. I needed a few drinks to feel confident enough to talk to a girl I liked. I needed to be buzzed to speak up in social situations. Alcohol had become my social lubricant, my liquid courage.

It's so easy to see the red flags now. Blackouts were becoming increasingly frequent. So were risky behaviors, like the time I ended up with blood all over my face with no recollection as to how after a drunken hookup, or the night I slept in a bed soaked with piss because neither I nor my partner could wake up enough to deal with it. These weren't just wild college stories; they were signs of a serious problem brewing under the surface.

But at the time, it all seemed normal. At Syracuse, what I was doing didn't seem that crazy. Everyone was getting wasted all the time, everyone was trying different drugs, and everyone was trying to figure out where they belonged. That's just college, right?

The whole time this was going on, I never thought I had a drinking problem. Not once. I mean, I had insane stories from when I was hammered. Some were funny, but others were pretty messed up. I always just wrote it off as "college life." I was young, having fun, and still managing decent grades.

Now, looking back as a forty-year-old guy with years in recovery, I can see all the warning signs. The blackouts, the risky behaviors, using alcohol as a social crutch and emotional band-aid—these were all early signs of the struggles I'd face later. But at the time, I was living in the moment, enjoying the freedom and possibilities that college offered.

I was creating an identity for myself, separate from the struggles my family faced back in Pittsburgh. I was Carl from Syracuse, the life of the party, the guy who could drink anyone under the table and still ace his exams. He was the cool guy everyone loved.

As graduation approached in May 2007, I felt unstoppable. I had survived four years at one of the top party schools in the country, kept decent grades, and was ready to take on the world. Over the years at Syracuse, I decided to try my hand at acting instead of pursuing a career as a sports reporter. I had a degree from one of the best communications schools in America, and I was ready to chase my dreams in Hollywood.

So I threw some stuff in a duffel bag, grabbed my guitar, and got myself a one-way ticket to LA. That was my master plan right there. I had about $600 to my name, and my credit card was totally maxed out, with a limit of around $1,000 or something. This kid from Syracuse said I could crash at his place for a few days, but honestly, I hadn't thought much past that.

Looking back, yeah, that was pretty stupid. But at the time, I thought, *This is going to be epic.*

Honestly? I hadn't thought any of it through. I booked that one-way ticket when I was hammered. It was a pattern that would follow me to the West Coast, where I used alcohol to numb my fears and push me forward, even when I wasn't sure where I was headed.

What I didn't realize was that I was also carrying with me a relationship with alcohol that would shape the next decade of my life. The coping mechanisms I'd developed, the reliance on alcohol for social confidence, using substances to handle stress and emotions, all of this came with me as I stepped into the "real world."

My time at Syracuse had transformed me in ways I couldn't yet understand. It had educated me, yes, but it had also introduced me to the party culture, the drinking, the drugs. It had all become so normal that I couldn't see how it was affecting me.

Getting on that plane to LA, I was pumped and clueless. I thought I was done with all the college craziness and ready to be a real adult. But really, all that baggage was coming right along with me, just stuffed in there with everything else I was chasing.

The next few years were gonna be all over the place—some incredible highs, some brutal lows, and through all of it, I'd be drinking more and more. But that's a whole other story.

Sitting there on that plane, man, I felt like anything could happen. The whole world felt wide open as if I were finally heading toward something big.

The real education, the hard lessons about addiction, about myself, about what truly mattered, was still to come. Syracuse had been the beginning, the first step on a long and winding road that would eventually lead me to recovery, self-discovery, and a life I couldn't have imagined.

But sitting on that plane watching Syracuse get smaller below me, I had no fucking clue what was coming. I was a twenty-two-year-old with a communications degree and a drinking problem I didn't recognize yet, heading to LA with barely enough cash to last a week. If someone had told me where the next decade would take me, I'd never have believed them. But that's how it goes, right? You think you're writing one story, and life hands you a completely different plot.

Chapter 3

WHEN I STEPPED OFF the plane at LAX in the summer of 2007, I experienced an intense mix of anxiety and grandiose ideas that only a kid with dreams of making it big in Hollywood could have.

I pictured LA as a promised land where I could transform from Carl Radke, the kid from Pittsburgh with the troubled family, into Carl Radke, the next big thing in Hollywood. In my mind, I saw myself quickly climbing the ranks, perhaps landing a few acting gigs, and eventually becoming a hotshot producer or director. Man, was I naive, ambitious, and unprepared for what was to come.

My first experiences in Los Angeles were a wild mix of highs then brutal reality checks. The city was everything I'd imagined: palm trees everywhere, tanned, good-looking people, and an energy that seemed to crackle with possibility. However, it was also overwhelming as hell, expensive beyond belief, and fiercely competitive in ways I couldn't have imagined.

I quickly realized that having a degree from a top communications school didn't automatically open doors in Hollywood. It couldn't even pry them an inch. Instead, I found myself taking on a series of odd jobs to keep the lights on. My first real gig in the industry was as a runner for a production company called World of Wonder. For anyone unfamiliar with Hollywood lingo, a runner is essentially the bottom of the food chain, the person with a car who does whatever they're told, from dropping off scripts to picking up lunch orders.

That first week in LA was a lot to take in. I was sleeping on a couch at a fellow Syracuse alum's place, but after about two weeks, he told me I couldn't stay anymore. Talk about being thrown into the deep end. Through a series of connections—a friend from Pittsburgh, who knew a guy who knew a guy—I ended up crashing at the home of a former NFL player in Santa Clarita, a suburb north of Los Angeles. His parents had a beautiful ranch with a guest room, and they generously let me stay there while I figured my shit out. The commute was brutal, but I was grateful to have a roof over my head.

The job at World of Wonder was far from glamorous, but it gave me my first taste of the industry. I was running scripts to Tori Spelling's house in Beverly Hills, picking up tapes from Bravo's offices, and getting a behind-the-scenes look at how TV shows were made. It was exciting, don't get me wrong, but I was making about $25,000 a year in one of the most expensive cities in the country. When I ended up on Bravo years later, some of the people I met back then were still working the same job. One guy I kept in touch with from those days told me recently, "I cannot believe that skinny kid with the surfer hair hustling around the office is now on our network."

I was so broke that I devised a system for stealing lunches from the production office. I'd be in charge of ordering food for the crew, and I'd add a fake name to the list, then take that extra meal home for dinner. Not my proudest moment, but when you're that hungry and broke, your moral compass gets a little wonky, you know?

In those first weeks in LA, I got my first (and only) DUI, something I should have taken as a massive warning sign. I had been out at a club in Hollywood with friends, drinking heavily as usual. I parked my car with the valet at the club, and when it was time to leave, I didn't hesitate to get behind the wheel. I was wasted, but in my mind, I'd done this before and had been fine.

As I turned onto Hollywood Boulevard, I cut off a police car like an idiot. I remember frantically putting pennies in my mouth because I'd heard somewhere that it would mask the smell of alcohol. I failed the field sobriety test right outside the nightclub, where I could hear the bass still thumping from inside as they arrested me. They took me to Van Nuys County Jail. It was my first time in a cell.

That night in jail was one of the most sobering experiences of my life, which was ironic, as I was coming down from being completely wasted. I remember sitting there, the cold concrete bench underneath me, surrounded by people who looked like they'd been through this many times before. I was scared shitless but also experiencing deep shame. Two female friends who were with me that night ended up bailing me out the next day. They never even asked for the money back; that's the kind of friends I had, better than I deserved at the time.

The DUI should have been a wake-up call, but instead, I saw it as bad luck. I ended up having to go to classes every Saturday for six months, got specific insurance, and lost my license for a while, though I'll admit I drove illegally because I felt I had no choice with work. The whole experience was brutal, but even then, did I think I had a problem? Not a chance. It was just "a bad night."

Following the DUI, I threw myself into work but still kept partying, though I knew I had to be careful as I needed to keep my job.

After six months at World of Wonder, I began to feel disillusioned. The runner job wasn't teaching me much, and I wasn't making connections that would help me advance my career. Then, one day, checking that same Syracuse alumni message board again (seriously, that thing was a lifeline), I saw a posting for a production assistant position on NBC's *Heroes*. This was a whole new level of TV production. The scale was massive, more like a blockbuster movie than a TV show. I nailed the interview, with a Syracuse alum, of course, and thought I'd finally made it.

But then disaster struck. The Writers Guild of America went on strike, and everything came to a halt. Suddenly, I was unemployed in a city where I was barely scraping by to begin with. But here's where the hustle mentality that's always been part of my DNA kicked in. So I'm hanging out at my friend's place and I see they've got all this firewood just sitting around their ranch. I asked them what they were going to do with it, and they said nothing really. That's when it hit me. I went on Craigslist, looked up what people charged for firewood, borrowed his dad's truck, and started a little business delivering wood around LA. We made almost $25,000 in a month and a half. Not bad for a guy who was desperate enough to steal lunch a few months earlier.

When the strike ended, I landed a job as a production assistant on *Criminal Minds*. Working on a hit network show like that was equal parts exciting and exhausting. I got to deliver scripts to Shemar Moore, Thomas Gibson, and Mandy Patinkin. I was working with stars I'd grown up watching. But the hours were ridiculous. I'd get to the studio at six a.m. and leave at midnight or one a.m. every single day. That's not an exaggeration. That was the standard expectation, and you didn't dare complain.

The job was demanding, but I was good at it. People liked me. I was that energetic PA who would get your coffee just how you liked it, remember your lunch order, and be there with a smile, even after fourteen hours. But underneath that helpful exterior, I was struggling. The stress, the pressure, and the long hours all started taking a toll. And that's when my drinking, which had already been pretty bad in college, started to get worse.

The high-stress environment of TV production created a culture where substance abuse was, if not encouraged, at least tolerated. People drank on set (low key, of course), smoked weed between takes, and did cocaine to stay awake during those grueling night shoots. I started doing cocaine to keep up with the demands of the job. At first, it was to stay awake during long nights in the production office. But soon, it became a regular part of my weekends too. I told myself it was just part of the Hollywood lifestyle, that this was what successful people in the industry did. Classic denial.

Working those long hours had one unexpected benefit: I was so busy that I didn't have much time to party. For a while, my work schedule kept my drinking and drug use somewhat in check, at least during the week. It was the weekends when things would go off the rails.

My relationships during this time were equally chaotic. The long hours and unpredictable schedule made it impossible to maintain an everyday social life. When I did go out, it was usually to industry parties or bars where networking was as important as socializing.

That's when I met her, a gorgeous young woman from a wealthy family. Let's call her "Skywriter Girl" (that's what the *Summer House* fans know her as). She came from serious money; private plane kind of money. We connected instantly, and I became completely infatuated with her. She was beautiful, confident, and from a world I'd only seen in movies. Dating her felt like I was finally "making it" in LA, albeit in a weird way.

We drank a lot together—like, *a lot*. Our relationship had an intense up-and-down pattern that always seemed to revolve around alcohol. She wanted to get serious fast, talking about marriage way earlier than I was comfortable with. Even so, there was something about her that kept me hooked, even as the pressure to settle down intensified.

We had explosive arguments that always seemed to happen when we were drinking. During one nasty fight, she even threw my dress shoes at me. Eventually, things came to a head at a wedding in Napa Valley, where, after another massive scrap, her dad had to intervene. We broke up the next morning, but had to take her family's private plane back to LA together. Awkward doesn't begin to describe it.

After that breakup, I went on what I can only describe as a rampage: drinking, partying, hooking up with anyone who would have me. I was trying to drink away how much that breakup sucked. Spoiler alert—that just made everything way worse.

At the same time, I was continuing to audition for roles, trying to break into the acting side of the business. But my anxiety and lack of preparation meant I rarely performed well. I'll never forget the audition for *Criminal Minds*, where Jason Alexander from *Seinfeld* was directing it. I was so fucking nervous I thought I might actually shit myself. Not exactly the smooth, successful actor I thought I was going to be when I moved out here.

The irony wasn't lost on me that I was working on this hit show and couldn't even land a small role on it. It was a humbling experience that forced me to take a hard look at what I was doing with my life. I remember looking out the window at *Criminal Minds* one day and seeing a woman who had been in the industry for twenty years driving up in her beat-up Honda Civic. She was still grinding, still struggling after two decades. That was a wake-up call.

I wondered if I had the skills, talent, or connections to succeed in Hollywood. I was auditioning and bombing. I was working these grueling hours for not much money. Meanwhile, my coping mechanisms, alcohol and drugs, were becoming more of a problem than a solution.

It was around this time that I had a conversation with the executive producer of *Criminal Minds*, a former Chicago cop who hadn't started writing until his thirties. He told me he wouldn't recommend my path, working up from PA. He'd had life experience, stories to tell. That conversation stuck with me.

Things were getting difficult, and I started to think that maybe there was another path for me that would provide me with some actual business skills and financial stability while I figured out what I wanted.

My dad was shocked when I told him I was thinking of leaving. "What? You're going to leave Hollywood?" He couldn't believe I was considering stepping away from the industry I'd been so passionate about.

The irony was that I loved telling people I worked on *Criminal Minds*. It was the ultimate ego boost when I'd go home for the holidays. "What are you doing now, Carl?" "Oh, I work on *Criminal Minds*." It sounded so cool. But the reality was I made $25,000 a year, worked exhausting hours, and was miserable a lot of the time. So, I made the difficult decision to leave Hollywood for a new job in a different industry.

Looking back on my time in Los Angeles now, I see it as this crucial chapter in my development. I didn't become the Hollywood star I thought I would, but I learned invaluable lessons about hustle, resilience, and what I was willing to sacrifice for success. I also got my first real glimpse at how destructive my relationship with alcohol and drugs could be, though it would take me many more years and many more rock bottoms to confront that problem fully.

I tried for years to get as many accolades in LA as I could, but my DUI, failed relationship with Skywriter Girl, and inability to nail auditions had all shown me that this path wasn't working. So, I headed back to the East Coast, ready to be closer to home and to settle down, but that's not what happened.

Chapter 4

LEAVING HOLLYWOOD WASN'T THE big mic-drop moment you might think. It was more like I slowly started realizing that this thing I'd been chasing since college wasn't working out. Those super long days on *Criminal Minds*, constantly trying to hustle for the next gig, feeling like I was getting nowhere—it all just started getting to me. I found myself questioning if this Hollywood thing was really what I wanted anymore.

Everything changed during a random weekend trip to Newport Beach. I'd been grinding away on *Criminal Minds* for a while, and although it was fucking cool to be part of such a popular show, the reality of those long hours and a pathetic paycheck was hitting me hard. In Newport, I met these sales guys who seemed to have it all figured out—making serious money, working when they wanted to, and actually getting to enjoy the good life instead of just grinding all the time.

As I listened to them discuss their careers, I couldn't help but compare them to my own situation. One person mentioned that he was making $300,000 a year, working four days a week, with an expense account and time to play golf on Fridays. Another guy had just started and was already pulling in $100,000. Meanwhile, I was barely scraping by despite working on a hit TV show. The contrast was brutal.

Here I was, supposedly living the "dream" in Hollywood, but I was broke as hell, stressed out of my mind, and not developing any actual skills I could use elsewhere. The idea of a stable career with room to grow and a decent paycheck was starting to sound increasingly appealing.

When I told my dad I was thinking about leaving Hollywood, he was shocked. Like, genuinely couldn't believe it. This has been my dream since I was in college. We'd invested so much time, money, and energy to get me to this point. However, I tried to explain that I needed to learn how to be a genuine "career person" to develop skills that would benefit me in the long term.

My dad, always the wise one, introduced me to the concept of the "learning-earning curve." He emphasized the importance of continuing to grow professionally while also earning a living. Looking at my situation through this lens, I realized that while I was definitely in the "learning" phase in Hollywood, the "earning" part was severely lacking.

After years of hustling in LA, working various jobs on different sets, I was barely making any progress. Meanwhile, these sales guys were crushing it. They had nice apartments and nice cars and didn't need to steal lunch from work like I did. When the guy told me they hire ex-athletes and competitive people, I thought, "Hell, that's me."

I made the tough call to leave *Criminal Minds* after season three. It wasn't easy walking away from the prestige of working on a hit show. I knew that when I went home for the holidays, I wouldn't have that cool factor of being able to say, "I work on Criminal Minds." But I also knew that the cool factor wasn't paying my bills or setting me up for any real future.

I landed a job with this medical company in Orange County and dove headfirst into their intense sales training program. It was boot camp in cold calling and persistence, making one hundred calls a day to complete strangers. At first, it was terrifying. I was used to being on set, surrounded by the controlled chaos of TV production. Now, I was sitting in an office, picking up the phone over and over, facing rejection after rejection.

As harsh as it was, it turned out to be what I needed. For the first time since moving to LA, I was developing marketable skills. I was learning how to communicate effectively, how to handle rejection, and how to close a deal. These were skills I knew would serve me well, regardless of where my career went next.

The learning curve was steep. I'd never been in a professional office environment before. I'd never had to wear a suit and tie every day. I had no clue about corporate politics or any of that stuff. But I wanted to make it work, you know? So I just threw myself into it. I'd stay up reading all the product manuals, practicing my pitch in the mirror like an idiot. Slowly, I started feeling like maybe I could do this.

Except my substance abuse continued to grow. During that time, I'd drive from LA to Fresno—about a four-and-a-half-hour drive—for work meetings, doing cocaine the entire way to function. I knew it wasn't right, but I couldn't stop. The only way to turn it off was to use it all up.

In spite of my vices, my success in sales led to a promotion and a move to Richmond, Virginia. The company thought I had potential and wanted to send me to this territory where they needed someone good. It felt like I could finally start over, you know? Get away from all the LA bullshit —the failed acting career, the drinking, all the disappointments. I was excited about this opportunity, ready to throw myself into something different and prove I could make it work.

But man, getting used to everything wasn't easy.

Moving from California to Virginia was a culture shock. The pace of life, the people, the weather; everything was different. I went from living in a beach town surrounded by the entertainment industry to a much more traditional city. However, something was refreshing about that simplicity and normalcy. For once, I wasn't constantly surrounded by people chasing fame, wealth, or status. I could focus on doing my job well and building something stable.

Except life has this funny way of throwing curveballs when you least expect them. The day before I left for Richmond, I met a woman. We spent twelve hours together, and I completely fell for her. Suddenly, I found myself in this long-distance relationship, flying back and forth between Richmond and California. After about ten months, I decided to move back to California to be with her.

Moving back to California wasn't just about the relationship. I missed the energy of the West Coast, the sunshine, the laid-back vibe. I missed being close to friends I'd made there. Fortunately, I was able to find a position with another medical company in California, and then we ultimately broke up. I was still drinking, but I was focused. I was building momentum in my sales career, and it felt good to have some professional stability even as my personal life was in flux.

This brings us to what happened in the Bahamas, the incident that turned my whole world upside down and sent me spiraling in ways I never saw coming. This was 2009, and I was on one of those company trips they do when you have a good year. President's Club trips, they called them, were if you crushed your numbers, they'd send you somewhere fancy and pick up the tab for everything.

I had invited a woman I'd just met in Pittsburgh to join me, a decision that, looking back, was reckless and fueled by my increasing alcohol use.

I'd met her at a club in Pittsburgh while visiting home. She was working as a bottle girl, and we hit it off. In my drunk, impulsive state, I invited her to the Bahamas with me. The next day, she wanted me to talk to her mom first, which should have been a red flag indicating how young and inexperienced she was. I was so caught up in the moment, the idea of having a hot date for this trip, that I didn't think twice. So I called her mom, and she told her daughter that I sounded like a nice guy, so she agreed she could go to the Bahamas with me.

On our first night at the resort, we were in our hotel room, the balcony doors open to the warm Caribbean night. The TV was playing music, and we were feeling good, riding high on the excitement of being in that beautiful place. Things were getting pretty intense between us, but then I started getting this weird feeling. Like someone was watching us.

I looked up and there a guy was standing on our balcony, watching us. He was peeking around the curtain, staring right at us. I couldn't make sense of what I was seeing. My brain just kind of stopped working for a second. It was like, this can't be real, right? This kind of shit doesn't actually happen. It felt like something out of a horror movie.

What happened next went by so fast, but I remember every single detail. I jumped up and started yelling at this guy. He freaked out when he realized I'd spotted him and tried to get away by climbing over to the next balcony. I ran to the window, still screaming at him, my heart going haywire. For a second, I couldn't see him anymore, but I could hear him struggling with the railing, trying to get over.

Then, an eerie silence. It couldn't have lasted more than a few seconds, but it felt like forever. That silence was shattered by the most horrific sound I've ever heard: the impact of the man's body hitting the ground twelve stories below.

The immediate aftermath was complete chaos. I was completely out of it, trying to wrap my head around what happened. I called the front desk, but I couldn't even get the words out right—I was babbling. I looked over the balcony and there he was. Just lying there with blood all around him. I can't get that picture out of my head. Even now, it's burned in my mind.

The police arrived, and our hotel room became a crime scene. They separated me from the young woman I was with and questioned us individually. I found myself trying to explain what had happened, still not fully comprehending it myself. The whole thing felt like I was watching it happen to someone else.

One detail that haunts me is that there was some blood on our sheets—not from anything sinister, but from hooking up. But right then, all I could think was that they were going to blame me for that guy dying. I mean, how do you even explain something like that? The whole thing was just insane and terrifying.

As the night progressed and the police continued their investigation, we learned more about what had happened. The man's name was Robert McNeil; he was forty-three, from North Carolina. The police found evidence in his room—porn magazines, an open laptop—that suggested this wasn't his first time being a voyeur. His wife and kid were supposed to have joined him that day, but hadn't arrived for some reason.

The police investigation revealed he had moved from balcony to balcony. He went from his room to another room and then to mine. He was essentially balcony-hopping to watch people. When they showed me his driver's license photo and asked if I'd ever seen him before, I could truthfully say no. He was a stranger who had made a fatal, terrible choice.

The next morning, still reeling from the events of the night before, I had to attend a company meeting. I was late, stumbling in as the president was giving his speech. When he asked if anyone had any comments, I knew I had to speak up. Standing before 150 of my colleagues, I explained what had happened. The room fell silent, everyone staring at me like I had three heads.

The company was supportive, telling me to take time off if I needed it. But instead of processing what happened in a healthy way, I found a colleague who had cocaine and spent the next few days blasted out of my mind. I buried the trauma deep inside, unable to manage with what had happened. It was easier to numb myself than to face the reality of what I had witnessed. This incident cranked my already problematic substance use into overdrive.

The woman I'd been with left pretty much right away—I mean, who could blame her? Her mom was losing her mind about the whole thing, and she just wanted to get the hell out of there. Whatever we had going on, it didn't survive this nightmare. So there I was, trying to cope with all of that on my own.

When I finally returned home, my parents came to pick me up at the airport. I had to tell them what happened, and I'll never forget the looks on their faces—a mixture of horror, confusion, and concern. They didn't know what to say or how to help me handle something so bizarre and traumatic.

The cops cleared me completely. They figured out that McNeil's death was an accident—he did it to himself, trying to get away. But knowing this didn't ease my conscience or help me sleep at night. I couldn't shake the feeling that if I hadn't been there, if I hadn't invited that woman, none of this would have happened.

I received a text from someone at the embassy in the Bahamas asking if I'd be willing to speak with McNeil's family. My lawyer advised against it, and honestly, I couldn't bear the thought of it. How could I possibly explain to his family what had happened? What would make any of this make sense?

Online news articles were published about the incident. The comments sections were full of speculation from people suggesting there must have been foul play, that there was more to the story, that McNeil couldn't have just fallen. Reading those comments was torture. I wanted to scream at these strangers who knew nothing about what had happened, who had no idea about the bizarre, tragic reality of that night.

I left the company soon after, unable to face the memories associated with that trip. I moved back to the East Coast, taking a job in Philadelphia with my former company. They took me back without hesitation, which was a lifeline I desperately needed at that point.

My drinking and drug use, which had already been problematic, spiraled entirely out of control. I was using substances not just to party or socialize but to numb myself, to forget.

Once, I had to drive to an important client meeting. I'd partied all weekend and hadn't slept Sunday night. Monday morning, I showered, put on a suit, and got in my car with a huge bag of coke. I did bumps the entire drive up, had the meeting in a completely wired state, then did more coke on the whole drive back. It was insanity, but I couldn't stop myself.

What made it even harder was that my dad asked me for money during this time, which I later found out was to help him get his own apartment as he was moving out of the house he shared with my mom. He presented it as "taking some space," but my mom later discovered he'd been having an affair. The betrayal cut deep, not just for her but for me, too. I was stuck in the middle, pissed at my dad but not wanting to blow up our relationship completely.

Between what happened in the Bahamas, drinking and using more than ever, and my parents splitting up, everything was hitting me at once. I was losing it, getting wasted more and more, to not think about all the shit that was happening. The young, ambitious guy who had moved to LA with dreams of making it big in Hollywood was gone, replaced by someone I barely recognized.

It took years of therapy, support groups, and hard work to process not just the trauma of that night in the Bahamas but all the underlying issues that had led me to that point. I had to confront the insecurities and fears that I'd been running from for so long.

Discussing the Bahamas in therapy was brutal. I had to go through every single detail of that night multiple times. All the feelings that came up—feeling violated, the shock, the guilt, being scared out of my mind. The hardest part was learning that McNeil's death wasn't on me. That took me a long time to actually believe.

The process of healing wasn't linear. There were steps forward and steps back. There were days when I thought I had moved on and days when the memories would hit me like a freight train. There were periods of clarity followed by periods of relapse. But gradually, with persistence and support, I began to put the pieces of myself back together.

To anyone dealing with trauma, particularly when substances are involved, I'd say this: Don't try to bury it. Don't think you can drink or drug it away. Seek help. Talk to someone. It's okay not to be okay. Healing is possible, but it requires facing your demons head-on.

The experience of the Bahamas has made me a strong advocate for mental health awareness and support, especially in environments where substance use is common. I've learned that trauma doesn't discriminate—it can happen to anyone, regardless of their circumstances. Talking about it and meeting other people who have been through similar experiences helps. Not just them, but me too.

I mean, I wouldn't want anyone to go through what I went through, but I've tried to make some sense of it. It taught me a lot about setting boundaries and taking care of myself—things I probably should have learned way earlier. It definitely allowed me to empathize with other people who've been through traumatic stuff and are dealing with it. It was a big part of figuring out how to get clean and understanding myself.

Every day, I choose recovery. Every day, I strive to be a better version of myself. Every day, I'm grateful for the second chance I've been given. I'm still figuring things out, you know? There are good days and bad days, but honestly, I wouldn't change any of it. All the stuff I've been through, the things I've learned about myself, the people I've met along the way—that's what makes me who I am now.

If you're out there dealing with trauma or addiction or whatever, just know that it can get better. It won't be easy, and there's no magic fix, but it's worth fighting for.

Chapter 5

AFTER WHAT HAPPENED IN the Bahamas, everything just fell apart. Coming back to Philly, I was barely functioning. I mean, how are you supposed to deal with watching someone fall to their death right off your balcony? That image stays with you. In the weeks after, I couldn't do anything normal. I'd be sitting somewhere, and then boom—my brain would take me right back to that hotel room, to that sound. God, that sound.

My work took a nosedive. I'd show up late, usually hungover, and my sales numbers went in the toilet. That drive I'd always had? Gone. My boss pulled me into his office multiple times, and I'd make these empty promises to get my act together. That job I'd been so excited about now felt like a massive weight I was dragging around.

The medical device company I worked for was initially quite understanding. They were aware of the Bahamas incident and gave me some space to process. But their patience had limits. After my third missed client meeting in a month, my boss sat me down for a "serious conversation." He used phrases like "performance expectations" and "professional standards" while I nodded along, promising to do better. I even managed to pull it together for a couple of weeks after that—showing up on time, making my calls, hitting some modest sales targets. But it was like trying to run with a broken leg. I was going through the motions.

Instead of getting help for what I now know was PTSD, I doubled down on partying. Drinking, which had already been a problem, became my daily crutch. I'd have a drink in the morning to steady my hands, then spend nights going from bars to clubs to after-parties. Cocaine became my constant companion because it kept me awake, kept me social, kept me from dealing with the shit storm in my head.

My apartment in Philly became a sad bachelor pad: empty liquor bottles piling up, takeout containers everywhere, laundry I couldn't be bothered to do. I'd sometimes go days without cleaning anything. Friends would stop by and give me concerned looks, but nobody really said anything directly. They could see I was going downhill fast, but nobody knew what to say to me. And honestly, even if they did, I wasn't going to listen.

I started hanging out with people who drank as much as I did. Anyone who tried to tell me I had a problem? I cut them out. I couldn't deal with people calling me out or trying to get me to get help. At that point, drinking wasn't about having fun anymore—it was just how I got through the day. Weekends weren't fun; they were non-stop benders, where I'd drink from Friday night until Sunday afternoon with barely any memory afterward of what had happened.

I'd meet random characters at bars, other functioning alcoholics who had their own demons to drown. We formed intense bonds that lasted as long as the bender we were on. We'd exchange numbers, swear we'd hang out again, but it was all bullshit. We were using each other to normalize our own destructive behavior. "See? Other successful people drink like this, too."

My old college friends tried to reach out to me. A couple of guys from Syracuse who knew me before all this would call or text, trying to check in. I'd avoid them for weeks, then randomly respond at two a.m. when I was wasted, sending long, rambling messages about how great everything was going. They'd try to follow up the next day, but I'd ghost them again. The thought of facing people who knew the "old Carl" was too much.

I became reckless as hell. Driving when I shouldn't, getting into pointless bar arguments, and waking up in random places with zero clue how I got there. My career goals seemed meaningless. Who cared about sales targets when life could end so suddenly? I had vague ideas about starting something in the hospitality or entertainment industry, but I was drifting. So I asked my boss if he would let me work in New York City.

The money situation got bad. Despite having a sales job that paid generously, I was spending way beyond my means. Bottle service at clubs, $200 bar tabs on weeknights, $80 Ubers when I was too drunk to drive, plus *all* the cocaine—it adds up fast. I started to rack up credit card debt, bounce checks, and dodge calls from bill collectors. I'd tell myself I'd figure it out later, that the next commission check would solve everything.

Dating became an endless cycle of short hookups. I'd meet someone, charm them for a few weeks, then bail before they could get close enough to see the mess I really was. It was easier to be around new people who didn't know about my past, who wouldn't notice how much I'd changed. And I gravitated toward other party animals, so the relationships were built on shared hangovers rather than actual connections.

There was a woman named Melissa, whom I dated for about two months, which was the longest relationship during this period. She was bright, fun, and had a great job in the fashion industry. On paper, she was perfect. But she also started noticing my drinking patterns. One Sunday morning, after I'd shown up to brunch still drunk from the night before, she sat me down for "the talk." She told me she was worried about me, that she cared about me, but couldn't watch me self-destruct. I vowed to cut back to get it under control. Two days later, I was blackout drunk on a Tuesday, calling her at three a.m. She stopped answering my calls after that. I can't blame her.

The blackouts got scarier and scarier. Entire nights, sometimes whole weekends, were completely gone from my memory. I'd laugh it off, play it like it was all part of having a good time, but deep down, I was terrified. The thought of facing life sober felt impossible, though.

Health-wise, I was falling apart. I'd gained weight from all the drinking and late-night food. My skin looked like shit. I was constantly battling a low-grade hangover that never fully went away. Sometimes, I'd get heart palpitations that frightened the hell out of me. I started popping Advil like candy for the constant headaches. My body was sending warning signals that I just kept ignoring.

It was in the middle of this shitshow that the *Summer House* opportunity landed in my lap. I was at my dentist's office, getting a cleaning, when Dr. Martin casually mentioned that my friends Kyle Cooke and Everett Weston were going to be on some Bravo show about the Hamptons. Curious, I fired off an email asking about this "Montauk thing." Everett responded that the producers were looking for one more guy and asked if I'd be interested in speaking with them.

The timing felt weirdly perfect. The idea of a fresh start, even if it was only for a summer on camera, was appealing. Plus, there was this small voice in the back of my head saying maybe this could be the beginning of something new—a pivot away from medical sales into entertainment or media.

I'd met Kyle and Everett the previous summer in the Hamptons. Kyle and I bonded over this outrageous attempt to pour a six-liter bottle of rosé at Surf Lodge. Classic Hamptons nonsense. Back then, I'd do an incredibly obnoxious thing: I'd buy a six-litre bottle of rosé and then challenge guys to pour the massive bottle one-handed, because I knew I could. When Kyle approached me, I forced him to participate. Kyle's hand shook so badly he nearly dropped the thing, but it was one of those drunk bonding moments that cemented a friendship.

Kyle had a big personality—confident, entrepreneurial, and always the center of attention. His energy pulled people in. I admired how he could work hard during the week, then party like a maniac on weekends, and somehow still have his shit together. We quickly became friends, spending most of that summer hanging out at the same spots, chasing the same women, living that classic Hamptons lifestyle.

Everett and I connected differently. His military background and the charity he founded for veterans really resonated with me. My family has a military history, and I've always respected the people who served. His work with veterans dealing with PTSD resonated with me, given what I was going through after the Bahamas, even though I wasn't addressing it.

Everett had a grounded quality that was rare in the Hamptons scene. When he talked about his experiences overseas or the veterans he worked with, there was a depth there that cut through all the superficial bullshit. We'd sometimes break away from the group at parties and have honest conversations. He was one of the few people I felt I could be authentic with, even though I never actually opened up about how much I was struggling.

We'd all become part of the same Hamptons crew. Weekends were often blurry marathons of beach parties, clubs, and overpriced dinners. Beneath all the surface-level partying, though, real friendships were forming.

Everett set up the call for me with the *Summer House* producers, and when I spoke to them, I turned on the charm hard. I sold them on Carl Radke—the successful medical device salesman who worked hard during the week but partied harder on weekends. Good-looking, single, outgoing. I conveniently left out the part where I was barely hanging onto my job, drowning in debt, and using substances to numb myself daily. They seemed to like what they heard, and within a week, I was signing contracts and preparing to have my life filmed for a national audience.

The idea of spending a summer in the Hamptons, partying with friends on camera? Equal parts exciting and terrifying. Part of me worried about exposing my struggles to the world, but another part hoped this might force me to get my shit together.

I convinced myself this could be a turning point. Maybe having cameras around would make me more accountable and force me to pull back on the drinking and partying. Maybe being around new people in a different environment would give me the fresh start I needed. This could even lead to a new career path, such as one in entertainment or media—so many maybes, all of which let me avoid the truth that I needed actual help.

I threw myself into prep mode, so I hit the gym harder than I had in years and blew money on new clothes. The shopping sprees were therapy. I'd spend hours buying outfits that screamed "successful and put-together guy." If I looked the part, maybe I could become it.

I dropped almost $2,000 on new clothes in one weekend—designer jeans, button-down shirts, swimwear, and shoes. Money I didn't have. I justified it as an "investment" in my future. This was my big chance, and I needed to look the part. The credit card debt could be dealt with later, after I became a reality TV star.

The gym became my temporary refuge. For those hours I spent working out, I felt like I was doing something positive, making progress. I'd push myself to exhaustion, partly to look good on camera but also because it gave me a brief respite from the chaos in my head. Sometimes, I'd even skip the post-workout drink, convinced I was making progress.

Mentally, I tried to pump myself up for the experience. In my head, I'd be this charming, funny guy with ambition and depth. I made all these promises to myself, like I'd control my drinking, showcase my professional side, and form connections with my housemates. I know now it was classic addict behavior, setting myself up for a dangerous game. The party boy image had become so central to my identity that I didn't know who I was without it.

I practiced what I'd say if the Bahamas incident somehow came up and rehearsed my backstory to edit out the messier parts. I created a whole narrative about myself as an ambitious, successful person, having fun while building my career. I believed my own bullshit to some extent. If I could convince viewers, maybe I could convince myself, too.

As filming approached, my emotions were all over the place. I hoped being on the show would help me reclaim the confidence I'd lost. Underneath, though, I was terrified people would see through the mask and that my alcohol issues would be exposed for everyone to see.

I also worried about living with a group of people under constant surveillance. What might slip out when my guard was down after too many drinks? There were so many things in my past that were still a closely guarded secret I hadn't processed myself, let alone shared with others. The thought of it being caught on camera made me sick.

Work became another source of anxiety. I hadn't exactly been employee of the month lately, and now I was asking for multiple weekends off to film. My boss wasn't buying it, but he said it was fine, as long as my numbers improved. I told him all this stuff about how I could handle both things, no problem. But I already knew that wasn't going to happen.

Despite all this, I was determined to make the most of it. The night before filming, I barely slept, my mind racing with questions. Would people like me? Could I keep it together on camera? Would everyone see through my bullshit?

I called my mom that night, trying to sound pumped but not too crazy about it. I didn't want her freaking out, so I played down all the drinking and focused on how good this could be for my career. "It could lead to other things, Mom. Connections in media and entertainment." She was cautiously supportive, but I could hear the concern in her voice. She knew me too well and could probably sense I wasn't in a great place, even through my upbeat disguise.

When morning came, I started packing for the Hamptons. Every item felt loaded with meaning—clothes, books (mostly props, if I'm being honest), even my grooming products. Everything was a statement about how I wanted to be perceived.

I snuck a bottle of vodka into my suitcase, telling myself it was just for pre-games in the bedroom before filming—a security blanket. I wasn't planning to get wasted on camera; I just wanted to take the edge off. Another lie I told myself. I also packed some Adderall, not my prescription, bought from a friend, to help me stay sharp and counteract the alcohol.

This decision to be on *Summer House* would eventually lead to my rock bottom, but also, ultimately, to my recovery. The party persona I was so desperate to maintain would become a prison of my own making, one that would take years to escape.

The drive out to the Hamptons that first weekend was surreal. I kept oscillating between excitement and panic. I'd been out there many times before, but always as just another partier. Now, I was going to be one of the cast members of a show, someone people would recognize.

Walking into the *Summer House* for the first time was unreal. The cameras, the crew, all these gorgeous people; it was overwhelming. I put on my best smile, cracked some jokes, and faked the confidence I wished I had. Seeing Kyle and Everett was a relief in this unusual new reality.

The production team provided us with a brief overview of how filming would proceed, specifically, which areas would be equipped with cameras when crews would be present and what was expected of us. They emphasized that we should be ourselves and live our lives as normally as possible. I remember thinking, *If they only knew what normal looked like for me these days.*

As I met the rest of the cast, I slipped into the role I'd prepared. Charming, outgoing, ready to party. It felt good to be that person, even if part of me knew it was an act. The house was exactly what you'd expect: a massive Hamptons mansion with a pool, hot tub, and plenty of space for debauchery.

I claimed a bedroom, unpacked my things, and immediately scouted the alcohol situation. The kitchen was fully stocked with beer, wine, and liquor. Relief washed over me; at least I wouldn't have to worry about maintaining my supply. I grabbed a beer, telling myself I'd pace throughout the weekend. One beer turned into shots, then more beer, then whatever else was being passed around.

That first weekend, I just threw myself into all the partying. I flirted with the women in the house, played drinking games with the guys, jumped in the pool fully clothed at one point: classic party Carl behavior. The cameras followed it all, and instead of making me self-conscious, they gave me permission to be more outrageous. This was what I was there for, right?

Then Sunday would come around, and I'd have to get back to the city, and everything would hit me like a truck. The hangovers were getting worse—not just physically feeling like crap, but mentally too. Sitting on that train back, head pounding, I knew I was heading down a bad road. I'd managed to hold it together for the cameras, but barely. I was one bad day away from completely losing it. The drinking had been even more intense than expected, and I'd come dangerously close to losing it more than once.

I scrolled through my phone, looking at the pictures from the weekend. In every shot, I had a drink in my hand. I looked happy, surrounded by beautiful people in a stunning place, but there was something hollow in my smile that I wondered if others could see. For a brief moment, I considered whether this whole thing was a mistake. But then I got a text from Kyle about plans for the following weekend, and I was right back in, already looking forward to the next party.

Back in the city, I went straight to my apartment and crashed for hours. When I woke up, the emptiness hit hard. After the constant stimulation of the house—the people, the action, the cameras—being alone with my thoughts was jarring. I grabbed a beer from the fridge to take the edge off, telling myself it was just the "hair of the dog" to cure the hangover.

Monday morning came too quickly. My boss asked how the "TV thing" went, and I gave a sanitized version: great house, cool people, very tasteful. I promised it wouldn't affect my work performance. Another guarantee that would never happen.

The week dragged by as I counted down to Friday when we'd all head back out to the Hamptons. Work was just something to get through, a necessary evil between weekends of filming. I found myself caring less and less about my sales targets or client relationships.

Every Sunday, as the train pulled into Penn Station and I prepared to step back into my real life, all I could think about was when I'd be heading back out to the Hamptons to do it all over again.

What I didn't realize was that the cameras would capture my unraveling in real-time, documenting my journey toward rock bottom for the world to see. But strangely enough, that public exposure would become part of my salvation. Sometimes, you need to see yourself at your worst to find the motivation to change.

Chapter 6

THE HAMPTONS. BEAUTIFUL BEACHES, crazy parties, and way too much drinking—that's where this whole mess went down. When I watch those early *Summer House* episodes now, it's wild how different things looked on TV compared to what was actually happening inside me behind the scenes. The show made it seem fun and glamorous, but what was unseen was that I was falling apart. This show is about the friendships that changed my life, hitting absolute rock bottom and somehow finding my way to recovery through it all.

My friendship with Kyle began after we met in the Hamptons before we appeared on *Summer House*. While that brief interaction with the rosé was the start, we began to run into each other in New York City at the Equinox, meeting there at ungodly early hours and pushing each other through these brutal workouts. We'd be drenched in sweat, still catching our breath in the locker room, and Kyle would start riffing about his latest business idea. The guy's brain never stops. His entrepreneurial energy was infectious, and I found myself drawn into his world of ambitious dreams and grand visions.

Back then, we were both deeply immersed in New York nightlife. We'd start at one bar, then club hop until four a.m., chasing the next thrill, the next party, the next round of shots. Looking back now, I can see we were laying the groundwork for all the issues I'd face later on. But at the time? Man, we were living the dream.

Our pre-Hamptons friendship was a perfect storm of work hard, play harder. We'd crush our sales numbers during the week, close deals, hit targets, and then completely let loose on weekends. There was an unspoken competition between us about who could party more intensely while still maintaining their professional edge. Neither of us realized we were playing a game that was dangerous.

After Everett's introduction to the *Summer House* producers and being cast, I still remember receiving the official call. I was walking down Park Avenue, phone pressed to my ear, trying to play it cool while internally freaking out. I immediately called Kyle, who was already confirmed for the show.

"Dude, we're actually doing this," I said.

"This is going to be epic," he replied.

From those early episodes, Kyle and I were tight. I remember our second weekend of filming, standing on the deck with the ocean breeze, looking at the chaos unfolding in the house, and exchanging that "what the fuck did we sign up for?" look that made us both lose it laughing. No matter how crazy shit got, we had each other's backs.

Kyle and I always confided in each other. Kyle opened up about his parents' expectations, and I shared some things about my brother's struggles that I rarely discussed. That kind of genuine connection was rare on reality TV.

But relationships in that house? Total minefield. The pressure cooker environment of having cameras follow your every move, being stuck with the same people weekend after weekend, and drowning it all in alcohol was the perfect recipe for drama and bad decisions.

My situation with Lauren Wirkus was a complete mess. The attraction was real; she was gorgeous, full of energy, and a lot of fun. However, our on-again, off-again romance was a disaster that played out for everyone to see. Having people in the house commenting on our relationship, plus millions of viewers picking apart every interaction, was way too much. I wasn't emotionally equipped to handle a normal relationship, let alone one under that kind of microscope.

Lauren and I had a magnetism that would pull us back together even when we knew better. We'd have incredible nights where everything seemed perfect, and then three days later, we'd be in screaming matches that the whole house could hear. The cameras captured everything, which only made things more intense.

We couldn't just have a private conversation to work through issues because every discussion became a scene, and every argument became fodder for content.

The worst part? I kept sending mixed signals because I couldn't be honest with myself about what I wanted. One weekend, I'd be all in, making her feel like this could be something serious, then the next, I'd pull away and act single. Looking back, I was unfair to her. My issues with commitment and substance use made me incapable of being a good partner, but I wasn't self-aware enough to recognize that at the time.

Then there was Stephen McGee. We'd stay up until sunrise, doing shots and having so much fun, but we connected on a deeper level. Stephen had this way of calling me out on my bullshit that nobody else would dare to. He pushed me to talk about things I'd rather keep buried. That dynamic eventually led to one of the worst moments of my time on reality TV.

Stephen and I had a complicated relationship where we'd bounce between being super close friends to barely speaking.

As the seasons stacked up, the drinking got out of control. Weekends in the Hamptons were built around alcohol—mimosas at breakfast, beer by the pool all day, shots before going out, more drinks at the club, then after-parties back at the house. For someone like me who already had issues with moderation, it was like throwing a match on gasoline.

I can still taste the tequila shots we'd line up on the kitchen island. That burn hit my throat, the momentary relief as my anxiety faded away, the false confidence that made me think I was killing it when I was a mess. Each weekend became a blur of parties and fights and hookups, all fueled by booze.

Our call times for filming would sometimes be ten a.m. on Saturday after we'd been out until three a.m. the night before. The crew would arrive, and we'd all be tired and hungover, so we'd make Bloody Marys or mimosas to start off the day. By noon, we'd be drinking full force again, starting the cycle all over. The cameras were always rolling, catching every sloppy moment, every regrettable comment.

The pressure to be "Carl the Party Boy" was relentless. Every stumble, every slurred word, every embarrassing moment—the cameras caught it all. I kept telling myself that this was my role, that it made good TV. Meanwhile, I was spiraling hard.

I'd wake up so many mornings with my head pounding, my mouth dry as hell, piecing together fragments of what happened the night before. The shame would hit me, but instead of facing it, I'd grab another drink to numb it out. It was this vicious cycle I couldn't break free from.

What viewers didn't see was how often I'd hide in the bathroom, splashing water on my face, giving myself pep talks to make it through another day of filming. I'd stare in the mirror, barely recognizing the bloodshot eyes looking back at me, and think, *You can do this. Just get through this weekend.* Then I'd pop an Advil, put on my sunglasses, and head back out to party.

Trying to balance my actual career with *Summer House* became impossible. I'd leave the Hamptons, still half-drunk, and then try to transform into a professional medical device salesman by Monday morning. The whiplash was extreme—one day, I'm funnelling beers in a flamingo float, and the next, I'm in a suit talking about dental equipment with doctors who have no idea what I did all weekend.

My Monday morning routine became a desperate attempt to piece myself back together. I'd wake up at six a.m., still not fully sober from the weekend, chug water and coffee, take the longest shower possible, and try to look presentable. I'd rehearse my sales pitches in the Uber on the way to meetings, praying my clients couldn't smell the weekend seeping out of my pores.

It started showing in my work. I'd arrive at meetings hungover, hiding behind sunglasses, pounding coffee to stay alert. My presentations got sloppy. My follow-up was inconsistent. I'd miss important emails because I was too busy checking social media reactions to the latest episode. The double life was catching up to me.

My boss started noticing. At first, it was just little things like "Everything okay, Carl?" Then it got more serious—"Your numbers are in the toilet." I'd promise him I'd get my shit together, focus more, figure out how to balance everything. But as the show started getting bigger, I was getting sucked into all of it without even noticing. I was hooked on that feeling.

Then came the call that I knew was coming but still shocked me: "Carl, today is your last day." Getting fired hit me like a punch to the gut.

I remember sitting in my apartment after that call, surrounded by *Summer House* promotional materials and sales documents, thinking, "What the fuck do I do now?" My identity had been so tied to being this successful sales guy who also happened to be on a reality show. Now, half of that equation was gone, and I had to figure out who I was supposed to be.

One of the most challenging moments during those early seasons was when a personal story about a sexual experience from my past was brought up on camera. The lights felt too bright, the silence too heavy, and I froze, unsure of what to say or do. I felt blindsided entirely and exposed in a way I never agreed to.

I'll share more details later on, but Stephen shared something on camera that I had told him in confidence during one of our late-night conversations. It wasn't his story to tell, and I hadn't given him permission to for it to become a storyline. When it happened, I felt a rush of emotions—embarrassment, betrayal, and anger—and I shut down. I couldn't handle it, so I just walked away. What else was I supposed to do?

That whole thing really messed me up. It was like getting slapped in the face with the reality of what this show actually was. Nothing was off limits to these people, not even your most personal stuff. Even people I thought were my friends would throw me under the bus for a good storyline. I learned real quick that I had to protect myself better, even from the people I was living with.

The aftermath was brutal. I had to watch that moment air months later and then deal with the public reaction, the articles, and the tweets. My parents saw it. My friends from home saw it. It's one thing to choose to share your own story; it's another to have someone else decide that your personal life should be entertainment.

Over those first few seasons, I watched myself transform from Carl Radke, the sales guy who liked to party, into "CARL FROM *SUMMER HOUSE*"—a larger-than-life character who was always the drunkest, the rowdiest, the most out of control. The worst part? The line between the character and the real me started to blur.

I became known for my crazy antics, my hookups, and my ability to party harder than anyone else. The audience ate it up, and I fed into it more and more. The pressure to maintain this image was exhausting, but I didn't know how to be anything else at that point.

Sometimes, the real me would peek through—late-night conversations with Kyle about our dreams or vulnerable moments when we talked about my family. But those quiet, authentic flashes usually got overshadowed by the shots, the arguments, and the messy drama that made for better TV.

The social media aspect made everything more intense. Suddenly, I had tens of thousands of strangers commenting on my behavior, my relationships, and my appearance. Some weekends, I'd be so anxious about how I'd be portrayed that I'd drink even more heavily, creating a self-fulfilling prophecy where my anxiety about looking bad on camera made me behave worse.

Summer House took over my personal life. Every relationship was put under an intense microscope. My relationship with Lauren became a public spectacle that we couldn't navigate privately. We'd have genuine moments of connection that'd be ruined by explosive arguments with twenty people watching and cameras rolling. The real and the performative became impossible to separate.

Dating while on the show became a double-edged sword. If I met someone I liked outside the show, they'd either be intimidated by the TV thing or way too into it for the wrong reasons. Those genuinely interested in me for me would then have to deal with seeing me hook up with someone else on TV six months later.

My friendships outside the show also started falling apart. The filming schedule was intense, and my D-list celebrity status changed how people interacted with me. I drifted away from old friends who knew the real me and surrounded myself with reality TV people and hangers-on who reinforced all my worst behaviors.

I'd get texts from childhood friends saying, "Dude, that's not the Carl I know," after particularly foolish episodes. Instead of taking that as the wake-up call it should have been, I'd get defensive or ghost them. I couldn't handle anyone questioning the version of myself I was presenting to the world, even if that version was destroying me.

The drinking got so much worse during this period. The emotional toll of being constantly judged pushed me deeper into dependency.

There were mornings I'd wake up, and my hands would be shaking until I had a drink. I started hiding bottles around the house so I always had easy access. I'd pre-game before filming to "take the edge off, not realizing I was just digging myself deeper into addiction.

My lifestyle became increasingly destructive. I was living for the cameras instead of for myself. My physical and mental health took a serious hit, but I was too caught up in maintaining my image to care.

Through all this chaos, my friendship with Kyle continued to evolve. He became more than just my buddy: he was my confidant, sometimes my conscience, and occasionally the mirror showing me truths I didn't want to see.

We had a massive argument during season three. The house was tense, everyone was drunk, and Kyle just laid into me about my behavior. "You're better than this, Carl," he said, looking more disappointed than angry. "I know you are." That cut through all my bullshit defenses. Here was someone who actually saw something good in me when I couldn't see it myself.

Kyle was going through his own struggles with being on reality TV, which created a bond between us. We understood each other in a way most people couldn't. Sometimes, that meant enabling each other, but increasingly, it meant challenging each other to do better. He'd check in on me after particularly rough nights, make sure I ate something, and make sure I got home safely. Small acts of friendship meant everything in the chaos.

Then there was this one night where I completely blacked out. I woke up the next morning with no clue what had happened, sick to my stomach about what I might've done or said. Kyle found me basically having a meltdown and just sat there with me while I freaked out about it. He didn't try to fix it or tell me what I should do - he just stayed with me when I was losing it.

All of that stuff made us way closer than just being on a show together. Kyle became the guy who'd be pumped for me when things went well, but who'd also tell me straight up when I was being an idiot. What we had turned into something real—like actual friendship built on trusting each other and getting each other.

Even when we fought—and we had some epic blowouts—there was always an underlying respect. I knew that even if Kyle was pissed at me, it came from a place of caring. He wanted me to be the best version, even when I didn't care enough to strive for that myself.

When I watch those early *Summer House* episodes now, it's a lot to take in. I was growing up, but God, it was ugly and it hurt. The cameras caught everything—the good, the bad, all the stuff I didn't want to deal with about myself.

That's when it really hit me how fake everything in my life had gotten. I'd created a wild, party-boy persona who was always ready with a joke or another shot, always down for whatever crazy thing would get attention. But underneath that, I was dealing with profound insecurities, unprocessed trauma, and a growing dependence on alcohol and cocaine to numb everything out.

The person I created for the show began to consume my real identity. I'd find myself acting "like Carl from *Summer House*" even when cameras weren't rolling because I didn't know who else to be anymore. I was playing a character based on myself, but an exaggerated version that was increasingly detached from my core values.

Having cameras around 24/7 blurred the line between reality and performance for me. I started making choices based on what I thought would make good TV rather than what was good for me. This disconnect between the real me and the on-screen persona created an identity crisis that took years to sort out.

The role alcohol played during this time was massive. Being on *Summer House* allowed me to make my excessive drinking a standard for Carl, the party boy.

I think about how different things might have been if I'd addressed my issues earlier. If I'd had the self-awareness to see that I was using alcohol to mask deeper problems, or if I'd had the courage to step back when I felt things spiraling. But that's not how addiction works. You have to hit your bottom.

The biggest takeaway from my *Summer House* experience was realizing that external validation—the fans, the followers, the fame—none of it filled the emptiness I was trying to escape. It wasn't until I started looking inward and doing the hard work on myself that I found any real peace or purpose.

Those early seasons exposed all my weaknesses, challenged everything I thought I believed in, and nearly destroyed me. But they also sparked the journey that eventually led me to recovery and self-acceptance.

Chapter 7

THE *SUMMER HOUSE* CAMERAS caught all my drunk bullshit, the messy hookups, and me talking about wanting to be successful. But they didn't show what was really going on with my family behind the scenes. While I was getting my fifteen minutes of fame on Bravo, my family was falling apart in ways I didn't even fully understand yet. That stuff would end up being huge when I finally tried to get sober and figure out who I actually was.

For me, the revelation about my parents' marriage became another justification for my increasingly problematic drinking and drug use. During the early seasons of *Summer House*, I frequently cited my parents' divorce as a reason for my behavior.

In the early seasons of *Summer House*, I would say, "Well, my parents are getting divorced."

So that gave me the excuse to be a fucking dickhead to everybody? To drink and yell at people? No, that's not how it works. That was so wrong. I still feel terrible. I'd been justifying my behavior with these things going on at home. My brother has issues, my parents are getting a divorce. Whatever it might be. I always had a reason why I could drink or party to it.

My parents' divorce became a convenient shield—a way to deflect criticism for bad behavior while continuing to spiral deeper into addiction. It wasn't that the pain wasn't real; instead, I was using real pain as an excuse to avoid confronting my own issues. As I would later recognize in recovery, this pattern of deflection and avoidance had been central to my approach to difficult emotions throughout my life.

I carried deep resentment toward my father for years following the divorce. The betrayal felt personal—not just to my mother but to the entire family. The way my father had handled the situation, asking for money under partially false pretenses and presenting the separation as temporary when he was already committed to someone else, compounded the hurt.

I had a lot of resentment with my father for many years, and part of that was because I used it as an excuse to drink. The anger was eating me alive. It made me drink more and use more, and it pushed me further away from my dad. It was this endless loop—I'd get wasted to not think about how pissed I was at him, then I'd tell myself the drinking was okay because my family was so screwed up. Round and round it went. Meanwhile, the drinking and drug use made it impossible to truly process the emotions around my parents' divorce, keeping the wound fresh and the cycle intact.

This complex mixture of anger, hurt, and avoidance would continue for years until a pivotal moment at an unlikely venue—a Tony Robbins seminar.

In December 2019, at a Tony Robbins "Date with Destiny" event in West Palm Beach, I had what I'd describe as a breakthrough regarding my relationship with my father. A fellow attendee had gotten on stage with his father, with whom he'd had a fractured relationship, and worked through their issues in front of thousands of people with Tony's guidance.

I almost get chills thinking about it because it was such a powerful way to connect that they both were angry and had animosity. It was almost as if the son was forgiving the father, and the father was forgiving the son. The experience prompted me to call my own father that night.

I called my dad, "I love you, Dad, and, you know, I'm really sorry." I didn't go through what my dad went through back then. I never tried to put myself in his shoes, you know? He was trying to build a family with my mom and do everything he could to give me a good life. I just couldn't see all the work he was putting in for me. He put food on my table, he gave me opportunities, and he helped my life. He's a human being; he fucked up.

This moment represented a crucial shift in my perspective—from viewing my father as the villain in a straightforward narrative to seeing him as a complex human being who had made mistakes. It was the beginning of forgiveness, though the process would continue to unfold over the years.

The acrimony was only hurting me in the end, and it was killing me, actually. And I wanted to release that anger. The experience at Tony Robbins was also significant because it marked a week of sobriety for me—one of my first extended periods without alcohol as an adult. Taking a break from drinking allowed me to approach my familial wounds with clarity, giving me the emotional bandwidth to begin processing the pain that alcohol had long kept at bay.

In the years since that breakthrough, I've observed a transformation in my parents' relationship with each other. What had once been a source of pain has evolved into something healthier and more supportive despite the circumstances that led to their separation.

My mom has even spoken to the woman my father is with now. And I've warmed up to her a lot more in recent years. And I've removed a lot of that anger. This healing neither happened overnight nor was it a linear process. Letting go of bitterness toward my father and his new wife has been part of my broader journey of recovery. As I've worked to address my own addictions and destructive behaviors, I've gained perspective on how pain cascades through families and how forgiveness becomes essential to breaking unhealthy cycles.

I don't believe in cheating. I don't believe in having an affair. But I do think my dad made some pretty brutal mistakes, but my mom did meet a fantastic man afterward. My parents both remarried, so I now have a stepdad and a stepmom in the mix. It was initially weird getting used to that, but they're now part of my family. The fact that I can actually be okay with all these changes shows me how much I've grown up, not just from getting sober but just as a person.

My family dynamics have profoundly shaped my understanding of relationships and commitment. Having witnessed my parents' marriage end after thirty-four years and having witnessed my brother's struggles with addiction, I carry these experiences into my own relationships.

The fractured family foundation that I experienced has made me both more cautious and more intentional in my own life choices. Getting sober and fixing things with my family kind of went hand in hand. Working on one helped me work on the other.

All that pain from my parents splitting up? I used to use it as an excuse to be a mess. Now, it's actually taught me things—like what I don't want to repeat in my own life. I have learned firsthand how secrets and lies can create deep wounds and how addressing problems directly—rather than medicating them with substances—leads to authentic healing.

I've learned that forgiveness isn't just something you do once and you're done. It's something you have to keep working at. Forgiving my dad and being okay with how our family looks now—freed me from carrying around all that rage. That antipathy was a big part of why I was drinking and using so much. Letting go of it made everything easier.

I'm acutely aware of the patterns of addiction and unhealthy coping mechanisms that have run through my family. My brother's struggle with addiction stands as both a warning and a motivator for me to break these cycles.

I think a lot of addiction and mental illness is tied directly to your family and your genes. My hope and goal is to break the tradition in my family of alcoholism and mental illness and try and create another version of this family that understands that addictions are hard and people aren't evil. This awareness of family legacy shapes not just my approach to substances but my entire worldview. I recognize that the patterns established in families can persist for generations unless someone consciously works to break them.

But it's really, really hard, and it takes every single family member to be on board. Our family was completely and utterly affected by addiction. But we're still here, my mom, my dad, and I. And we're trying to move forward with positivity and live with purpose. Now I can see how both my mom and dad are building these new lives for themselves, but they're not just pretending the past didn't happen. They're showing me that even after something harrowing like a divorce, you can move forward and create something different without throwing away everything that came before.

The story of my family is not a neat narrative with a tidy resolution. We're all still figuring it out, you know? Everyone is changing and growing, and that affects how we all get along with one another. My parents' divorce felt like the end of the world when it happened. But looking back, it had to happen. The way our family looks now is totally different from when I was a kid, but it works. It's not what I thought I wanted, but it's good in its own way.

Trying to deal with all the family drama while also battling my drinking problem and being on TV? That was a lot. All the messy emotions from my parents' divorce would just spill over into how I acted on camera. I was hurting because of it, but I was also using it as an excuse to be a disaster.

However, going through all of that—the family mess, my own problems, everything tangled up together—it actually made me stronger. Being able to forgive my dad and accept how our family is now, while trying to have better relationships with everyone ... I had to grow up a lot. It wasn't easy, and it hurt like hell, but I did the work.

As I continue my sobriety journey, my evolving family relationships stand as both a testament to how far I've come and a foundation for where I hope to go. The family that once threatened to fracture beyond repair has instead reconfigured into something different but enduring—a testament to the resilience of family bonds even through the most painful transitions.

When I look back at the confused, angry guy using his parents' divorce as an excuse to misbehave on *Summer House*, I barely recognize him. That version of me couldn't see past his own pain to understand that everyone in my family was hurting in their own way. My mom, my dad, my brother—we were all just trying to navigate a situation none of us expected or wanted.

Today, I understand that family is both the foundation we stand on and something we actively build throughout our lives. The fractures in mine have gradually been filled with something new, not erasing the cracks but creating a stronger, more authentic connection because of them.

CAKE EATER

It's a work in progress, but then again, so am I.

Chapter 8

I'VE ALWAYS KEPT CERTAIN things private, which doesn't make much sense when you consider how much of my life I've shared on TV. I get how contradictory that sounds. I've talked about my breakups, my career falling apart, my family drama, and even my drinking and drug problems on camera. But there were still some parts of me that I wanted to keep to myself. Some things felt too personal, even for someone who basically lives their life in public. Not because I was ashamed, but because some experiences belong to you and you alone.

That changed during Season Two of *Summer House*.

Between seasons, I was hanging out with Stephen McGee. We'd formed a bond, not just as castmates but as friends who understood the strange new world we were navigating together. Being recognized on the street, seeing your life play out on TV, dissected by strangers on social media, it's a unique kind of pressure. Stephen and I would often blow off steam together—late nights, too much alcohol, lines of cocaine, and conversations that stretched until dawn.

One night, I shared a story from my past. I was twenty-two, fresh out of college and trying to break into acting in Los Angeles. I'd landed a role in a small theater production that was a collection of vignettes about casual hookups. The director had taken an immediate interest in me. At the time, I just thought he saw potential in me. Looking back, there were red flags from the beginning.

"Ooh, you're cute," he'd said during my first audition, a man in his late forties eyeing me like I was an item on a menu. "Take your shirt off." And I did because I was a twenty-two-year-old kid who wanted his big break. I didn't know any better. I didn't recognize what was happening.

After the show wrapped, we had a party backstage. I was blackout drunk, making out with the actress I'd been paired with in my scene. In the darkness, someone else joined us. It happened fast, and when I realized what was going on, I stopped it immediately, pulled up my pants, and left. I never spoke to either of them again.

This wasn't a story I told often; in fact, I'd kept it buried for years. But that night with Stephen, high on cocaine and drunk on whatever we were drinking, I mentioned it. Made a joke about it being "the best head I ever got." A throwaway line that felt safe in what I thought was a private moment between friends.

I never dreamed it would become a storyline.

The first hint that something was wrong came when Lauren told me Stephen had said something about me and another guy. I denied it outright, partly because I barely remembered telling Stephen and partly because I was blindsided that he would share something so personal with others. When you're in the reality TV world, you develop an intuition for potential storylines, and this had "ambush" written all over it.

I was *right*.

We'd been filming Season Two for a weekend when I got a text asking me to film with Stephen in Hell's Kitchen on Monday night. This wasn't unusual. We often filmed one-on-one conversations during the week. What was remarkable was walking into that bar and seeing not just Stephen but Ashley, Lauren's twin sister, waiting for me.

The cameras started rolling. Stephen brought up what I'd told him that night, suggesting I'd been lying about my sexuality. In an instant, a private moment became public property.

The feeling is hard to describe; that complete violation, that sense of your world collapsing around you. I managed to confirm what happened, but emphasized that it wasn't Stephen's story to tell. When the cameras stopped, Stephen broke down crying on the street. I walked away in shock, my mind racing and my body numb.

I went straight home and ordered alcohol and cocaine. I needed to escape the feeling of being exposed, of having my sexuality—something I'd never questioned—suddenly become a topic for public consumption. I was straight. I'd always been straight. I'd been taken advantage of in a vulnerable moment when I was young, and now I was being victimized again, this time for entertainment.

The fallout was immediate and intense. The storyline created a rift between Stephen and me for the rest of that season. I barely spoke to him, only having a final conversation when production filmed it. When the episodes aired, I had to relive the entire experience all over again, watching viewers speculate about my sexuality on social media.

Each time, I spiraled further. Each time, I drank more. Each time, I needed more cocaine to numb the feeling of being exposed.

What most people don't understand about addiction is that it's often tied to trauma. For me, that public questioning of my sexuality became a wound that wouldn't heal. I'd already been using alcohol and drugs to cope with insecurities, professional pressures, and family issues. Now, I had a new reason to escape.

The drinking got worse after that season. I became more secretive about it, more isolated. I had different groups of friends I'd party with, careful to keep them separate so no one could see the complete picture of how much I was using. I'd disappear from the *Summer House* crew for a night, only to show up the next day still wired from the night before, claiming I'd just had "a crazy night."

What really got to me wasn't just that my privacy got violated entirely—it was how differently I got treated because I'm a guy. If this had happened to a woman, if she'd been taken advantage of sexually and then had to talk about it over and over again, people would've been furious. There would have been support, protection, and people calling it out as wrong. But because I'm a man and because it involved another man, suddenly, it felt like it was okay to turn it into entertainment. It became something for people to gossip about and dissect on TV. The double standard was brutal—like my trauma mattered less because of my gender. That hurt almost as much as what actually happened.

In the years that followed, I built a protective shell around myself. I cultivated the "Carl the Party Boy" persona even more intensely; it was safer to be seen as the fun-loving player than to let people see the real hurt underneath. When you're the life of the party, nobody asks too many questions about why you're drinking so much. Nobody wonders why you need to escape.

The truth is, I wasn't drinking because I loved alcohol. I was drinking because I couldn't stand being sober with my thoughts. I was drinking because every time that storyline came up, I felt that same sense of violation all over again. I was drinking because it was easier than dealing with the fact that my sexual history had become public discourse without my consent.

It's hard to explain what it feels like to have your sexuality questioned publicly when you've never questioned it yourself. It's like having the ground shift beneath your feet. Suddenly, something you've always known about yourself—something fundamental to your identity—is up for debate. And not just among a close circle of friends but on national television, scrutinized by strangers on the internet.

I was already struggling with insecurities. Growing up, I was bullied about my appearance—my ears were too big, and my teeth were discolored. I was "Dumbo." I was "the nice guy," not "the hot guy." I carried those wounds into adulthood, into my time on reality TV, where every physical imperfection is magnified and mocked online. Having my sexuality added to the list of things people could speculate and joke about was unbearable.

And so I drank. I drank because it numbed the pain. I drank because it gave me the confidence to walk into a room and not care what people were thinking or saying about me. I drank because it was easier than confronting the complex feelings I had about what happened that night in Los Angeles—the confusion, the damage, the lingering sense that I had somehow brought it on myself by being so drunk.

It was really after that Season Two incident that my drinking patterns changed. It wasn't just about having fun anymore. It was only about escaping. I started drinking earlier in the day. I started drinking alone. I started making excuses to cancel plans so I could drink on my terms without anyone noticing how much I was consuming.

And what was I trying to escape? The shame. The feeling of being exposed against my will.

I grew up around people who were accepting of everyone, and I'm a supporter of the LGBTQ+ community. I genuinely believe people should love whoever they want to love and be whoever they are. That's always been my perspective on the world. So, when I was uncomfortable talking about my own trauma on national TV, it wasn't about anything other than protecting myself from having to relive something painful over and over again.

Because that's what it was—trauma. It wasn't until years later, in sobriety, that I could name it as such. A twenty-two-year-old kid, near-blackout drunk, being sexually touched by a man who had power over him professionally—that's not a consensual encounter. That's not a fun experiment. That's someone being taken advantage of when they couldn't properly consent.

But at the moment, I didn't have the vocabulary or the perspective to understand it that way. All I knew was that it was something I didn't want to talk about, something that made me uncomfortable, something I'd buried until that night with Stephen.

And when it was brought up on camera, I didn't just have to deal with it once. I had to deal with it repeatedly. First in the filming, then in the watching, then in the reunion, then in the press interviews, then in the random encounters with fans who felt entitled to ask about it. Each time, the wound reopened. Each time, I reached for the bottle, for the bag, for anything that would numb the pain.

The insidious thing about using substances to cope with trauma is that they prevent you from processing the trauma. You keep pushing it down, pushing it away, but it's still there, festering beneath the surface. And every time you're reminded of it, the pain feels just as fresh, just as intense, because you've never allowed yourself to work through it.

That's what was happening to me. I was living in this cycle of trauma and avoidance with alcohol and cocaine as my tools. And the longer it went on, the more I needed to consume to achieve the same numbing effect. That's how addiction progresses—what used to be enough isn't anymore, so you keep increasing the dose, increasing the frequency, chasing that relief that becomes more and more elusive.

There were moments of clarity, of course. Mornings when I'd wake up feeling so physically and emotionally awful that I'd swear off drinking and drugs. But by evening, the pain would return, the memories would resurface, and I'd be back where I started, reaching for whatever would make it stop.

I don't blame Stephen entirely for what happened. We were both young, both navigating a strange new world of fame, both using substances that clouded our judgment. He made a terrible decision, one that had profound consequences for me, but I can see now that he was operating within a system that rewards drama and conflict and treats people's personal lives as content.

What really got to me wasn't just that my privacy was infringed on; it was how alone I felt dealing with it. Having to discuss it over and over again on camera, turning it into something for people to discuss and analyze for entertainment, broke my heart. There wasn't the same understanding or protection that would exist in other situations. It became something for people to scrutinize instead of recognizing it for what it was. The whole thing left me feeling like my discomfort and boundaries didn't really matter.

I blame myself for how I handled what happened. I blame the way I turned to drinking and drugs instead of actually dealing with the pain. I blame all those years I spent running from something I should've been working through and healing from.

Drinking and drugs felt like they were helping, but they were making everything worse. Every drink, every line of coke, was just pushing me further away from getting better. I was dragging out the pain while telling myself I was getting relief. I wasn't healing anything.

It wasn't until I got sober that I could begin to untangle all of this. In sobriety, you have to face yourself, all of yourself, including the parts you've been running from. You have to sit with uncomfortable feelings instead of numbing them. You have to revisit painful memories without the buffer of intoxication.

And that's what I eventually did. I had to confront what happened that night in Los Angeles. The fact that I was taken advantage of, I didn't consent, and that it wasn't my fault. I had to confront what happened with Stephen and the betrayal, the public exposure, and the aftermath. I had to acknowledge how much those experiences had shaped my relationship with substances and how much they had fueled my addiction.

Only then could I begin to heal. Only then could I start to release the bitterness I'd been carrying—anger that had driven me deeper into addiction.

Stephen eventually reached out in 2021 with a long message of amends. He'd gotten sober himself, done the work, and reached out to apologize for what happened. At the time, I wasn't ready to deal with it. It took me until 2023 to finally respond to him. I accepted his apology and took responsibility for my part in things as well.

That exchange was healing. Not because it erased what happened but because it allowed me to release some of the anger I'd been carrying—pain that had fueled so much of my drinking.

Looking back now, I can see how that one storyline altered the course of my life. It accelerated my addiction at a time when I was already vulnerable. It created a wound that I tried to numb with more substances, which only made things worse.

This isn't just about what happened to me—I've seen this pattern on other shows too. When women go through trauma, people are more careful about how they handle it. They are protected from certain storylines and questions. People are more sensitive about it, and that's good because everyone deserves that kind of respect. But men also deserve that same respect. It's not about taking anything away from anyone else but more about recognizing that trauma is trauma, no matter who it happens to.

Being a public figure does mean your pain is often turned into entertainment. Your vulnerabilities are fair game. Your traumas are punchlines. And when you try to protect yourself, when you try to set boundaries, you're seen as problematic, as uncooperative, as not playing the game.

So you drink. You do drugs. You do whatever it takes to numb yourself enough to keep playing the game, to keep showing up, to keep smiling through the pain. Because what's the alternative? Walking away? Losing everything you've worked for?

That's the trap I found myself in. It's a situation that many men and women who've been assaulted fall into, not just those in reality TV. We're taught to be strong, to push through, to handle our own problems. We're not taught how to process trauma, how to heal from violation, or how to ask for the help and protection we need.

I don't want to be a victim in this story. I don't want pity. What I want people to understand is how one thing can completely derail your life for years to come. Having to talk about it publicly over and over again just makes the pain worse. When you're a guy dealing with trauma, people don't take it as seriously—they minimize it, make it seem like no big deal. And that just pushes you deeper into drinking and drugs because you feel like nobody gets it. I want people to see how that cycle works, how one bad experience can turn into years of destroying yourself because you don't feel like you're allowed to hurt the same way other people are.

Most of all, I want there to be change. I want the public to be more respectful of the issues brought up on reality TV, regardless of gender. I want there to be more awareness of how storylines about sexuality, sexual experiences, and private moments can cause real harm to real people. I want there to be more awareness of those struggling with the aftermath of such exposure.

That's what I want to be remembered for—not just getting sober but calling out the problems that push so many people to drink and use in the first place. Until we fix those problems, until people start treating each other with actual respect and getting real consent, there's going to be more people like me.

I'm one of the lucky ones. I got sober. I found healing. I rebuilt my life. But for every story like mine, dozens of others have yet to find their way out. And for them, for the ones still trapped in that cycle of pain and numbness, I'll keep telling my story, no matter how uncomfortable it makes people. Because they deserve better. We all do.

Chapter 9

LOOKING BACK, I CAN see how addiction crept into my life. It wasn't one moment where everything changed—it was a slow build, a gradual normalization of behavior that was anything but normal. In New York City, especially in the social circles I was in, drinking heavily and doing recreational drugs wasn't seen as an addiction. It was just what you did. It was the backdrop to everything—success, failure, celebration, commiseration. It was always there, woven into the fabric of my life so seamlessly that I couldn't see where the partying ended and the problem began.

When I first moved to New York, I was this kid from Pittsburgh with big dreams. I wanted to make it in sales, earn money, meet attractive women, and live the Manhattan life you see in movies. And for a while, that's what I got. But the city comes with a price. The pace is relentless. The competition is fierce. Everyone's trying to outwork, outplay, and out-party each other. That pressure cooker environment was the perfect breeding ground for my addiction to take root.

The truth is, alcohol was my gateway drug. I've always been the life of the party, the big personality in the room. I'm 6'5, loud, energetic; I fill a space just by existing in it. Drinking amplified that. It was liquid confidence to be the most exaggerated version of myself. When I was feeling insecure or anxious about filming, which happened more than I'd like to admit, alcohol was there to smooth those edges. It was my social lubricant, my crutch, my trusted friend that never let me down.

I remember when I first realized alcohol alone wasn't doing it for me anymore. I was at a party in the Hamptons, surrounded by people, drink in hand, and I felt... nothing. Flat. I needed something more to get that buzz, that release. That's how Adderall entered the picture. If you've never done it, Adderall is like flipping a light switch in your brain when you're drunk. You can keep going, keep drinking, stay sharper, and push through the fog that comes with heavy drinking.

It started casually—a friend offering me a pill at a party. "This will help you rally," they said. And boy, did it ever. I went from ready to pass out to the most charismatic guy in the room in about thirty minutes. I could drink more without feeling the depressant effects. I could stay up all night and still function the next day. It became my secret weapon for long nights of partying followed by early morning responsibilities. The pattern became predictable: drink to get loose, take Adderall to stay operational.

Adderall changed the game for me. It wasn't just recreational anymore; it became functional. I'd take it before filming sometimes, especially if I were hungover. I'd take it before important meetings or work events. I'd justify it by telling myself it was prescribed to millions of people. It wasn't like I was doing meth or heroin. It was just a little pill that helped me focus, perform, and be the Carl everyone expected me to be.

The irony is that I used to judge my brother for his addiction issues. I'd look at him and think, *That's not me. I've got my shit together. I'm successful. I'm on TV. I'm making money.* The denial was thick. I couldn't see that I was heading down the same path, just with a more socially acceptable package.

Cocaine was the final piece of my addiction puzzle. In New York, especially in the circles I ran in, cocaine was everywhere. It wasn't a sketchy activity like you see in movies. It was casual, like ordering another round of drinks. "Going to the bathroom" became code, and everyone knew what it meant. Lines were being done openly at parties in the Hamptons. People would share it as if it were no big deal.

The accessibility was shocking. I could order it like a pizza, and it would arrive at my door faster than the food would. Dead serious. And you get deals. You buy this, you can get that; a party special. Order the coke, and you'll get some Xanax the next day for the comedown.

My worst years were definitely seasons three and four of *Summer House*. Watching those episodes now is painful. I look physically ill. My face was bloated and pale, my eyes unfocused. I was agitated, aggressive, and unpredictable. I was spiraling but convincing myself I was fine. I'd watch the episodes air and think, "*That's not me. That's just a bad edit.*" But there's only so much you can blame on editing when the person on screen is clearly not well.

The daily cycle became routine. I'd wake up hungover, push through work, start drinking again in the evening, add Adderall to stay sharp, then cocaine to keep the night going. Rinse and repeat. On filming weekends, it was amplified. I'd show up to the house already buzzed, drink through the day, escalate at night, and often not remember what happened. The moral hangover the next day, that feeling of dread about what I might have said or done, became as familiar as the physical hangover.

The darkest moments were the ones alone in my apartment. I'd tell friends I was staying in, and what that really meant was drinking and doing coke by myself, listening to music, and watching TV until I inevitably started making phone calls at three a.m., scaring the people who cared about me. My dad got those late-night, tearful, incoherent calls far too often. I'd call him crying hysterically, not making sense, waking him up in the middle of the night with my emotional rollercoasters.

Those solitary binges were the most dangerous. There was no one there to tell me to slow down, to check if I was okay, to cut me off when I'd had too much. It was just me, my substances, and my increasingly dark thoughts. I'd do line after line, drink after drink, watching the sunrise through my apartment windows, feeling like absolute shit but unable to stop.

My addiction didn't just hurt me—it damaged relationships and hurt people who didn't deserve it. The whole thing with my castmate, Jules Daoud, at Kyle's birthday party, was me at my absolute worst, and it's probably one of the most embarrassing moments I've ever had on TV. I was dealing with this girl cancelling on me, feeling rejected and pissed off, but instead of handling that like an adult,

I took it out on Jules. I was wasted, and on Adderall, and when she came to me, trying to talk, being vulnerable, I exploded at her. Told her I didn't want her in the house anymore and accused her and another castmate, Jordan Verroi, of ruining our summer. The whole house was watching me have this meltdown.

Look, the alcohol and Adderall were talking, but I still said those words. I still screamed at someone who absolutely did not deserve it. That wasn't really me, but I have to take responsibility for it. It was cowardly—taking my pain about something wholly different and dumping it on her.

Watching that episode air was a wake-up call. I saw myself through the eyes of the viewers, and it was ugly. The comments online were brutal—deservedly so. But even that wasn't enough to make me stop. I apologized to Jules, felt terrible about it, and then went right back to the same behaviors.

When my castmate, Hannah Berner, mentioned on a podcast that I was doing Adderall, it was another turning point. When that reporter called asking for comment, "Hannah Berner was on Andrew Collins' podcast and said that you were doing cocaine and Adderall during the filming. Would you like to comment?"

I was furious. I texted Hannah: *Are you fucking kidding me? What the hell did you say on this podcast?* She responded that it was a joke, that everybody knows I do Adderall. But having someone else publicly say I was doing drugs for the first time felt like a betrayal.

Until then, my drug problem had been my secret, my issue that I could manage privately. But now it was out there, and people were talking about it. The shame was overwhelming. But again, instead of addressing the real problem, which was that I was abusing substances, I focused on being angry at Hannah for exposing me.

One of my cast members and I were evil influences on each other. We would drink in the car on the way to the Hamptons. We would drink on the drive home. We would stop for more drinks on the way back to the city. There always had to be drinks before leaving for the Hamptons. Our friendship was built on partying.

This pattern repeated in my relationships during those years—surface-level connections fueled by substances and the pursuit of attention. I was thirsty for validation, and none of it was healthy. I used relationships, fame, and attention as a substitute for another high.

Substances completely warped my state of mind during this period. I was paranoid at times, overly emotional, and quick to anger. The mood swings were extreme. I could go from being the life of the party to breaking down in tears in a bathroom stall in the span of an hour. The drugs were in control, not me.

The problem continued to escalate. There were moments when I'd done so much cocaine that I felt like my heart was going to stop. There were times I didn't sleep for three days straight. One night, after a drinking party, I lost consciousness and passed out for ten seconds in the back seat of a car. My friends got me Gatorade and water, and I somehow snapped out of it. Looking back, I should have gone to the hospital. I could have died.

The Christmas dinner incident was another low. I was in charge of cooking a pot roast. After drinking whiskey heavily, I got into an argument with my friend about the cooking time. I had a mini meltdown, said "fuck you," and stormed out. I went down to my apartment, called my dealer, ordered another bottle, and sat alone doing drugs. Some friends eventually came down to check on me, and instead of helping me, they joined the party.

When I showed up to the first BravoCon in 2019, I committed to not drinking. However, on the first night, I eventually started and ended up staying out until seven in the morning. The next day, I showed up hungover and tired, and by Sunday, I was still drunk from Saturday night. I got into an argument with a fan. I was fighting with people who wanted to take pictures with me at BravoCon. That's how bad it had gotten.

I took an Uber from New York City to the Hamptons during the COVID-19 pandemic because I was worried about being alone in my apartment. I knew what would happen if I was isolated—I'd drink and do coke until I couldn't anymore. At least in the Hamptons, I had a friend to stay with, which provided some structure and accountability.

I showed up to a family friend's dinner so drunk from the night before (and continuing to drink through the day) that I went upstairs, found their bed, and passed out. They had to wake me up when it was time for them to go to sleep in their own bed. It was embarrassing, but even that wasn't enough to deter me.

During all of this, I started working at Loverboy, the alcoholic beverage company Kyle began. I would show up to work fucked up sometimes in those first few years. Kyle and Nick were worried about me. My world was crumbling slowly, but I kept chasing the next high as if I could outrun the consequences.

There's a level of self-awareness in addiction that's particularly torturous. Part of me knew what I was doing was destructive. I'd have moments of clarity where I'd think, *This has to stop.* I'd moderate for a few days, maybe even a week. I'd hit the gym, eat healthy, and swear off the hard stuff. But then the weekend would come, or a stressful day at work, or a fight with a friend, and I'd be right back where I started, often worse because I'd try to make up for lost time.

Hiding it became an art form. I'd lie about how much I was drinking. I'd disappear to the bathroom at regular intervals and return with a burst of energy that I'd try to play off as natural enthusiasm. I'd cancel plans at the last minute when I knew I'd be too hungover to function. I'd deflect, minimize, and rationalize when friends expressed concern.

Professional consequences began to pile up as well. I was unreliable at work. I'd miss deadlines, show up late, and underperform. My sales numbers at Loverboy were suffering. I was letting down people who had taken a chance on me professionally. The anxiety about my career only fueled more substance abuse, and it was a vicious cycle I couldn't seem to break.

The thing about addiction is that it distorts your perception of reality. I convinced myself that I was still in control, that I could stop anytime I wanted, and that everyone else drank and partied just as hard as I did. I told myself that my job practically required this lifestyle—I was on a show about partying in the Hamptons, after all. What did people expect?

But deep down, I knew the truth. Normal people don't need to be drunk or high to interact with friends. Normal people don't hide bottles around their apartment. Normal people don't turn every social occasion into an opportunity to get wasted. Normal people don't wake up with crushing regret and shame multiple times a week.

The lies I told myself were elaborate and ever-changing, but they all served the same purpose: to keep me from facing the truth about my addiction. I wasn't a fun party guy who sometimes went too far. I was an addict using alcohol, Adderall, and cocaine to avoid dealing with my insecurities, my fears, and my unresolved traumas.

My relationship with my brother was complicated by addiction. He had been struggling with his own demons for years, and instead of showing compassion, I'd judged him. I'd spoken about his addiction publicly, disrespectfully, without understanding. The hypocrisy is not lost on me, now criticizing him while secretly battling my addiction.

When it comes to addiction, there exists a toxic idea of a "functioning addict." For years, I clung to that label. I still had my apartment, my job, my friends. I was on a TV show, for god's sake. How bad could my problem really be? But "functioning" is relative, and the bar kept getting lower. As long as I wasn't living on the streets or in jail, I could tell myself I was fine. But I wasn't fine. I was barely hanging on, putting all my energy into maintaining a façade while crumbling behind the scenes.

The thing about addiction that people don't talk about enough is the isolation. Even in a crowded room, surrounded by friends, even with hundreds of thousands of Instagram followers, I was profoundly alone because no one knew the real me.

I think about all the moments I missed, all the connections I failed to make, all the opportunities I squandered because I was drunk or high or hungover. I think about the honest conversations I avoided, the emotions I refused to feel, and the growth I stunted because it was easier to escape than to engage.

While I was staying at a friend's house in the Hamptons during the COVID-19 pandemic, I was supposed to be getting myself together, focusing on moderation. But I'd still have nights where I'd drink too much.

There were warning signs all the time, signals from my body and mind that I was pushing too hard. The anxiety that would grip me the day after a binge. The depression would settle in as the substances wore off. The physical tremors. The racing heart. The insomnia is followed by a crash lasting twelve hours or more. My body was begging me to stop, but I refused to listen.

Addiction is patient. It waits for moments of weakness, for excuses, for justifications. And I had plenty for all three. Every low point became a reason to drink more, to numb more, to escape more. It was a cycle I couldn't break because I wasn't ready to admit I was trapped in it.

For years, I lived in two realities: the public Carl, who seemed to have it all together, and the private Carl, who was falling apart. I was the life of the party, the guy everyone wanted to hang out with while secretly wondering if I'd wake up the next morning. That's the brutal truth of addiction: you're the star of the show, and everyone is applauding while the curtain falls.

Chapter 10

IT'S EXTREMELY TOUGH WATCHING yourself at your worst on national television. It's like seeing yourself with no filter—just exactly who you've become, whether you want to face it or not. Most people's rock bottoms happen behind closed doors. Mine got edited, produced, and shown to millions of people.

Season Four of *Summer House* started airing in early 2020, and I could barely stand to watch it. Each episode was like a horror movie where I was both the monster and the victim. I'd see myself on screen, eyes unfocused, words slurring, entirely out of control. I'd see the Carl who couldn't remember entire conversations, entire nights. The Carl who was spiraling and somehow thought more alcohol, more Adderall, more cocaine would solve the problem instead of being the problem.

Back then, I didn't have the words. I just knew I couldn't watch myself. The embarrassment was too much. The shame was overwhelming.

It wasn't just how I looked—it was how I was behaving. I couldn't stand myself. And if I couldn't stand myself, how could anyone else? The comments online confirmed what I already knew. People were disgusted by my behavior. They called me everything from a douchebag to a full-blown addict. They weren't wrong.

By the time Season Four was airing in early 2020, I was in what I'd later describe as arguably the worst I've ever been. I was financially in despair with mounting credit card debt. I'd shown up to work at Loverboy drunk or high, worrying Kyle and Nick. My world was starting to crumble slowly.

Then, when Hannah mentioned on a podcast that I was using Adderall, it was the start of everything coming to light. I got a call from a reporter asking for comment, and my entire world started to shift. Until that point, my behavior had been broadcast, but not the underlying cause. Now, people were talking about "Carl's problem" explicitly.

The world shut down due to the pandemic just as Season Four was airing, showing my worst behavior to a captive audience stuck at home with nothing to do but binge reality TV and judge. I was alone in my New York City apartment, isolated and anxious, watching myself spiral on screen as I spiraled in real-time. I couldn't face it. I couldn't face myself.

I had a friend in the Hamptons who offered his place if I needed to escape the city. Within days of the lockdown, I panicked at the thought of being secluded in my apartment, where I knew I'd just drink and do more cocaine. I called my friend and said I needed to come stay. I took an Uber from Manhattan to the Hamptons, a journey that, under normal circumstances, would have seemed crazy but, at that moment, felt necessary for my survival.

From March until the start of filming for Season Five, I stayed with my friend in the Hamptons. And something unexpected happened. Away from the city, away from my usual triggers and routines, away from the places I associated with partying, I found some breathing room. I found a space to start thinking about making changes.

I enrolled in this weekly wellness program, which was talking about drinking and alcohol. Or drinking and drugs. By no means was I saying I needed to get sober yet, but I was trying to be sober and seeing what would come of it, so I was doing meetings; I was going to that stuff each week.

It was my first attempt at something resembling recovery. Not a full commitment to sobriety—I wasn't ready for that yet—but a recognition that something had to change. I deleted Twitter. I removed the Instagram app after making posts to support the show, not allowing myself to look at the comments because they were brutal. I was getting absolutely abused on social media.

So, I just didn't look. I didn't engage. I focused on my own recovery and figuring out my life, all against the backdrop of a world that was suddenly uncertain and scary in ways none of us had experienced before.

Those months living in the Hamptons before Season Five started were transformative. I did not drink. I did not do cocaine. I did have "one or two moments" where I drank, but then I would be sober again for a couple of weeks. I was talking to a therapist who suggested that maybe moderation could work for me. It was the first time I was actually being honest with a therapist.

It was my first time doing therapy while actually telling the one hundred percent truth. I'd done therapy over the past six years, and I never once, up until that past January, admitted that I drank a ton, that I'd done drugs, that I'd partied way too much. It was liberating, opening up with this therapist who focused more on alcohol and just being completely honest about everything.

That honesty was a new experience for me. I'd spent years compartmentalizing, minimizing, and lying to myself and others about the extent of my substance use. I'd blamed relationships, blamed work stress, blamed anything but the real problem: me and my choices.

I was blaming girls in relationships. I was blaming other things except for myself. And after a while, you start pointing fingers. I started losing more friends. People were not wanting to hang out with me because I was a lot to be around.

For the first time, I was starting to face the truth about myself and my relationship with substances. It was painful but also, in some ways, a relief. There's a strange comfort in finally admitting what you've known deep down all along.

But I wasn't ready to commit to complete sobriety. The thought of filming Season Five completely sober terrified me. The thought of me just walking into season five without drinking totally was like a scary thought. How the hell can I film a reality TV show that I've never filmed before without alcohol? I couldn't imagine doing it. Alcohol had always been my crutch on camera, giving me the confidence to be louder, more outgoing, and more dramatic. You know, I always had this extra layer that I could drink on, more confidence. If there needed to be more drama, or more stuff, or talk more things, alcohol gave me that license to do that.

So, I went into Summer 2020 with a plan to moderate. I was going to drink, but I'd do it responsibly. I was going to show everyone how much I'd changed, how much work I'd done in those four months of trying to get my act together. For a while, it seemed like it might work.

I started dabbling; I'm only going to have Loverboys all night. I had some, I would say, successful nights, not getting too crazy. I didn't buy cocaine. I only drank. Passed out. It felt manageable. It felt like I was in control. I was being careful. I was thinking more about what I drank and how much I drank.

But moderation doesn't really work when you have addiction problems. You think you can handle it. You think you've got it figured out, but you're just fooling yourself. You might do okay for a while, but eventually, you're going right back to where you started.

Looking back, I can see that my first attempt at sobriety in 2020 wasn't going to work. It was a recognition that I had a problem, a desire to change, but not yet the full acceptance of what that change would require. I was still trying to find a middle ground, a way to have my cake and eat it too. I wanted to be healthier and more in control, but I wasn't ready to give up drinking entirely.

There was more to it than just the show. Drinking had become central to my identity. In New York City, I was known for buying bottle service at clubs. I was "the guy" who would get the table and bring the party. When I first moved to the city, day drinking was my thing—starting early, going all day, all night, and then waking up and doing it all over again. Alcohol and, later, drugs had been my way of fitting in since college.

So, the idea of being in that environment without drinking was almost unimaginable. Who would I be without alcohol? How would I fit in? How would I film a show that's fundamentally about partying without partying?

These were the questions I was grappling with in those months leading up to Season Five. I was doing the work—attending meetings, talking to a therapist, and trying to be honest with myself and others about my struggles. But I wasn't ready to make the full commitment to sobriety. I was still hoping there was a middle path, a way to control my drinking rather than eliminate it entirely.

It's easy to look back now and see how naive that thinking was. Addiction doesn't work that way. It's not something you can negotiate with or set boundaries around. It's an all-or-nothing proposition. But I needed to learn that lesson for myself through experience rather than being told.

The pandemic, in a strange way, had given me a glimpse of what sobriety could look like. Those months in the Hamptons, away from my usual triggers, had shown me that there was life without substances. I'd found moments of clarity, of peace. I'd started to rebuild some of the parts of myself that had been eroded by years of heavy drinking and drug use.

But the pull of old habits is strong. The fear of change is powerful. And the culture of reality TV, of New York nightlife, of the Hamptons party scene—it all pushed me back toward familiar patterns, even as I was trying to establish new ones.

One of the most complex parts of that first attempt at sobriety was the self-reflection it required. To truly address my relationship with substances, I had to look at why I was using them in the first place. What was I trying to escape? What was I trying to numb? What insecurities or fears was I trying to drown out with alcohol and cocaine?

The pandemic screwed with me in different ways. I was stuck alone, cut off from people who could help me, and I was anxious as hell—all the stuff that usually made me want to drink and use. But at the same time, I wasn't around all the places and people I normally partied with. I had to slow down whether I wanted to or not. I had to actually sit with myself and think about what was going on.

In all that stillness, I started thinking about how much drinking and drugs controlled my life. I was going to meetings, talking to this therapist who knew about alcohol problems, and for once, I wasn't lying about how bad things had gotten. It was progress, even if I wasn't ready to get completely sober yet.

The irony is that the pandemic, which brought so much suffering to so many, might have saved me from myself. If I had stayed in New York City, isolated in my apartment, I might have drank and used my way through those months, spiraling deeper into addiction. Instead, I found myself in the Hamptons, with a friend who offered support, in an environment that gave me space to start making changes.

It wasn't a straight path. There were setbacks. There were moments of weakness. There were those "one or two" times when I drank, breaking the streak of sobriety I'd been building. But the direction was clear: I was moving toward a healthier relationship with substances, even if I hadn't yet reached the destination.

As Summer 2020 started coming closer, so did the filming of Season Five, and I faced a new challenge. Could I maintain this more moderate approach to drinking in an environment that was designed for excess? Could I be the Carl people expected to see on camera while also being the healthier, more controlled Carl I was trying to become?

I went into that summer with a mix of optimism and fear. I was proud of the work I'd done and the progress I'd made. I was nervous about testing that progress in the pressure cooker of *Summer House*. I was hoping to find a balance and show a different side of myself on camera.

This first attempt at sobriety in 2020, imperfect as it was, represented a significant shift in how I viewed myself and my relationship with substances. It was the beginning of a recognition that the path I'd been on was unsustainable and that something had to change. It was a time of painful self-reflection, of confronting truths I'd been avoiding, of taking tentative steps toward a different kind of life.

I didn't know then where those steps would lead. I didn't realize that moderation would prove to be a temporary solution, not a permanent one. I didn't know that I had further to fall before I would find solid ground. All I knew was that I couldn't keep going the way I had been. The evidence was too clear, the consequences too severe.

So, I entered the summer of 2020 as a work in progress—still drinking but more mindfully, still using but more cautiously, still figuring out who I was without the constant haze of intoxication. It wasn't sobriety, not yet. But it was a start. It was the first acknowledgment that the relationship I had with substances was problematic, that it was affecting my life, my health, and my relationships in ways I could no longer ignore.

In the world of recovery, it is said that admitting you have a problem is the first step. In 2020, I took that step. I didn't immediately follow it with all the other necessary steps, but I had begun the journey. I had started to see myself clearly, perhaps for the first time in years. And that clarity, however uncomfortable, was the foundation upon which everything else would eventually be built.

It was a beginning, not an end. It was the moment when denial gave way to awareness and when avoidance began to transform into acceptance. It was the first time I considered the possibility that there might be a different way to live, a different Carl waiting to be discovered beneath the layers of alcohol and drugs I'd been hiding behind.

That possibility, that glimpse of a different future, was what I carried with me into the summer of 2020. It wasn't enough to keep me sober, not yet.

Chapter 11

WRITING THIS CHAPTER WAS one of the most painful things I've ever had to do. On August 11, 2020, my brother Curtis lost his life due to an overdose.

During this time, Curtis and I weren't in a great place. We'd always had a complicated relationship, but things had gotten especially tense in the last couple of years. I'd talked about his addiction struggles on the show, thinking I was being open about our family situation, but not fully understanding how much it hurt him to have his personal battles broadcast to the world.

Curtis had this idea stuck in his head about taking over our childhood home—the same place we'd been renting for $860 a month all those years. My mom was planning to move in with Lou, her soon-to-be husband, and Curtis saw this as his opportunity.

He'd just hit six months out of rehab, and things seemed to be looking up for him. He was getting his feet back under him, but based on his history, that stability was always fragile. Just when you'd think he was on the right path, something would trigger him, and he'd spiral again.

When he approached my mom about taking over the house, she hesitated. She knew the cycles all too well—the recovery, the relapse, the turmoil. She told him she didn't think it was the right time for him to handle that kind of responsibility. It wasn't what he wanted to hear, not by a long shot. He was hurt and felt rejected. That disagreement cast this dark cloud over what should have been a happy time for our family.

I tried to remain neutral throughout the situation. Part of me understood where Curtis was coming from—he wanted stability, a place that felt like home, a fresh start. But another part of me knew my mom was right. Curtis was still early in his recovery, and taking on a house, even our childhood home, might be too much pressure. I never told him this, though. I just listened when he called to vent, not wanting to damage our already fragile relationship.

Around this time, my mom was preparing to marry my stepdad, Lou. With COVID restrictions in full force, they couldn't have a big wedding back in Pittsburgh. It put me in a tough spot because I couldn't leave the *Summer House* cast without having to quarantine again, so I told her I'd watch via Zoom and stay in the Hamptons.

My friends and I gathered around to celebrate my mom's wedding through the screen. It was bittersweet, knowing that while it was great to see my mom happy, Curtis and his family didn't attend because of that argument about the house. Our family was fractured at what should have been a moment of joy.

I remember feeling torn that day—happy for my mom to find love again but heartbroken that our family couldn't all share in it together. As I watched her say her vows through a laptop screen, surrounded by cast members instead of family, the reality of how disconnected we'd all become hit me hard.

August eleventh was the day my world stopped spinning. The phone rang at seven a.m., and seeing my mom's name on the screen, I immediately knew something was wrong. A voice inside me whispered, "It's about Curtis," before I even answered.

When I picked up, my mom's voice was broken entirely. I could hear the pain in every word; *Curtis was gone.* I started crying immediately and couldn't stop. I was sobbing so hard I could barely breathe, and the sound was echoing through the whole quiet house. It felt like someone had just ripped my heart out. Everything was different after that moment. Everything.

It wasn't just being sad. It was like this huge hole where Curtis used to be. All our history together, the fights, the good times, all the complicated brother stuff—just gone. The world kept moving, but I couldn't. I was completely frozen.

I remember sitting on the edge of my bed, still holding the phone, unable to move. My body just stopped working. How the hell do you even begin to deal with something like that? How do you keep breathing when part of your foundation has been ripped away? Curtis wasn't just my brother—he was my first friend, my childhood rival, my reference point for understanding myself. Even with all our complications and distance, he was a constant in my life. And now he was gone.

I ran upstairs to find Kyle, desperate for someone to help me make sense of this nightmare. After I told him, we hugged, but nothing was going to make this better. I had to get outside and move, so I stepped out and called our executive producer. She got it—her brother had his own problems with addiction. She came right over, and we just sat on the porch crying together. No cameras, no bullshit, just two people dealing with something horrible.

The production team was exceptional. They shut everything down right away and focused on making sure I was okay. They never once tried to turn this into some storyline or content, which means everything to me. You hear about reality TV exploiting people's worst moments, but these people actually gave a shit about me as a human being.

Meanwhile, Kyle broke the news to the rest of the cast. As morning came, my housemates gathered around me outside. They formed a circle of support, not saying much because what the fuck can you say? But just being there for me.

I had to get away, even for a little while. I put on my headphones, blasting music that reminded me of Curtis, and just started walking. No destination, just one foot in front of the other through the streets of the Hamptons. I kept calling my dad, both of us trying to process this impossible thing that had happened, both searching for answers we knew wouldn't come.

The hours blurred together. I remember bits and pieces—sitting on a bench, just staring at the water, calling my sister-in-law and hearing how devastated she was, texting people back home who knew Curtis. Every conversation made it feel more real. Like, this was actually happening. Curtis was really gone. My friends, the crew, people who'd become like family over all these seasons - they were all there for me. The way they showed up for me was the only good thing I could feel right then. It made me realize that even when everything goes to shit, you don't have to go through it alone. We had this motley family, not blood but something else, something formed through all the crazy shit we'd been through together.

Luke, who'd gone through his own family tragedy, knew exactly what to do. He didn't try to offer empty words or awkward comfort. He was a steady presence, letting me know I wasn't alone. Paige made sure I ate something. Amanda quietly took care of practical details so I wouldn't have to think about them. Each person found their own way to help carry a tiny piece of this unbearable weight.

After getting the news, I knew I had to get back to Pittsburgh. Bravo was incredibly understanding, telling me to do whatever I needed to do. I got in the car and made the long drive home, my mind racing the entire way.

That seven-hour drive was one of the hardest things I've ever done. Alone in the car, memories of Curtis flooded back: road trips we took as kids, fights in the backseat, sharing headphones to listen to music. I thought about our last conversation and how mundane it had been. We'd talked about nothing important; we were just checking in. If I'd known it would be the last time we'd speak, I would have said so much more. I would have told him I loved him, that I was proud of him, that despite everything, he mattered to me.

Pulling up to my childhood house was surreal. My parents were standing together on the front porch—something I hadn't seen in years. They were united in their grief, there to support me and each other and honor Curtis. For a brief moment, we were a family again, brought together by the worst possible circumstance.

Walking into that house without Curtis there felt wrong. Everything reminded me of him—his favorite chair, the bedroom where we'd play video games, the backyard where we'd wrestle as kids. It was like entering a museum of our shared history, except one of us was permanently absent.

The funeral destroyed me. In giving the eulogy for my brother, I tried to capture who he really was to honor his memory properly. After the service, I couldn't handle the pain. I went straight to the bar next door with a friend and got wasted. It was a pointless attempt to dull everything I was feeling.

I stayed in Pittsburgh with my family for a few days, feeling Curtis's absence every moment. Then it was time to head back to the Hamptons, back to *Summer House*. Due to COVID protocols, I couldn't simply walk back into the house. I had to get tested and quarantine alone, just me and my grief. Those days were fucking heavy.

During that isolation, I kept thinking about a DM I'd received before filming started. It was from a girl who had been close to my brother. She wrote about their time together after rehab and how they'd become friends. It was this unexpected connection to a part of Curtis's life I hadn't been part of.

She shared stories about him that showed a side of Curtis I rarely got to see: his compassion for others struggling with addiction, his sense of humor even in recovery, and the way he'd go out of his way to help newcomers to the program. It painted a picture of my brother as a mentor figure, someone who used his own harrowing experiences to guide others. Reading her messages gave me both comfort and regret —comfort knowing he'd found purpose in helping others and regret that I hadn't been there to witness it.

I remembered struggling with the decision to meet up with him that summer. My mom had tried to set it up, but I chickened out. I told myself I wasn't ready, but the truth was I was scared. Our relationship had been strained for years, full of misunderstandings and resentment, especially about how we each handled our addictions. I'd talked about his struggles on TV, not fully understanding how much that hurt him, and he'd lashed out in response, creating this gap between us that seemed impossible to cross.

Looking back, the regret eats at me—all the things I never said, the chance to reconnect that I let slip away. My brother's anger came from a place of deep hurt, hurt that I contributed to. Now he's gone, and I'm still wondering what could have been if I'd just taken that opportunity to make things right.

Many people couldn't understand why I went back to *Summer House* after Curtis died. However, for me, there was a sense of commitment to the show and the group that had become such a significant part of my life. I needed to be there, to continue being part of something I cared about despite everything that had happened.

I genuinely believed Curtis would have wanted me back in that environment, surrounded by friends and the support of the *Summer House* cast. He wouldn't have wanted me sitting alone, drowning in grief. Being in that house, as crazy as it gets, somehow felt right. If I hadn't been part of that unique family, I would've been alone, trying to process everything by myself. The constant energy and presence of people who cared about me gave me something else to focus on.

This was when Ciara and I really connected. She was new to the cast but fit in immediately. Until that moment on the porch, after Curtis died, we'd never had a real one-on-one conversation. But that talk is something I'll never forget. She understood in a way that only comes from having your own painful experiences. That conversation made coming back to the house easier.

Tragedy creates these unexpected bonds. Ciara and I barely knew each other, but in that moment when I was completely broken, we connected. She didn't try to fix anything or tell me it would be okay. She listened to me fall apart. She let me be a complete mess without trying to make me feel better or judge me for it. There was no fake comfort and no trying to rush me through it.

So much happened between my return to *Summer House* and my finally getting sober, none of it good. All I wanted was to honor my brother and who he was as a person, but I was a fucking mess. The media created this narrative that I was handling his death so well, but behind the scenes, I'd slipped right back into drinking and doing cocaine just to function.

The truth is, I was drowning. Every smile for the cameras, every "I'm doing okay" was a complete lie. I'd wake up, take a shot just to steady my nerves, put on my mask for filming, then completely fall apart once the cameras were off. The show became both my escape and my prison—a distraction from grief but also a pressure to perform normalcy when I was anything but normal.

I started calling my parents at three or four in the morning after being up for days, high and drunk out of my mind. During those late-night conversations, I learned more about who Curtis had become toward the end.

My dad shared stories about Curtis in rehab and how he was always looking out for others despite fighting his own battles. He was administering Narcan, literally saving people from overdosing, pulling needles from the arms of those too far gone to help themselves. At forty-two, my brother was one of the older guys in there, sharing wisdom from a life lived the hardest way possible. Even in his darkest hours, his instinct was to help others.

One story stuck with me. Apparently, Curtis had talked a younger guy out of leaving rehab early. The kid was struggling, convinced he could handle things on his own. Curtis spent hours with him, sharing his own experiences and the consequences of leaving treatment too soon. That kid ended up staying, completing the program, and still sends my parents updates on his recovery milestones. My brother saved his life without ever knowing it.

That legacy—helping people even when you're in pain yourself—is something I knew I had to carry forward. Committing to recovery wasn't just for me; it was to honor him, to live a life that could make a difference, and to continue the work he couldn't finish.

Curtis dying changed everything for me, though it took months to really understand that. When I lost him, I started seeing what actually mattered—connecting with people for real, helping others, being honest about my problems instead of hiding behind bullshit. It's fucked up that it took losing my brother to wake me up, but sometimes that's just how life works. The worst things that happen to you end up being what changes you the most. The hardest moments become the catalysts for the most important changes.

Every day I work on my recovery, I think about Curtis. I think about the battles he fought, the demons he faced, the times he fell and the times he got back up. His struggle informs mine. His story is part of my story. And though he's gone, the impact he had on my life continues to shape who I am becoming.

Chapter 12

GRIEF DOESN'T WORK LIKE you think it will. You can't plan for it or control it. It just hits you and fucks up everything. After Curtis died, I thought I had some idea of what I was dealing with. I'd lost people before. I'd been through bad shit. But nothing prepared me for how losing my brother would transform me, how it would become both an excuse and a catalyst for the darkest period of my addiction.

When I returned to the *Summer House* after Curtis's funeral, I was greeted with cheers and hugs, a warm welcome back to this makeshift family that had become such a significant part of my life. I felt loved. I felt supported. For a brief moment, I felt like maybe I could push through this, honor my brother by living well, by staying on the path toward moderation that I'd been tentatively exploring before his death.

That illusion lasted about twenty-four hours.

The truth is, I used my brother's death as a VIP ticket back to party lane. All aboard. When the pain became too much to bear, which was nearly all the time, I turned to the familiar embrace of alcohol and cocaine. They were old friends, always there, always ready to numb the pain, to help me forget, if only for a few hours, the gaping hole that Curtis's absence had left in my life.

I left the Hamptons and went back to my SoHo apartment in New York City. That apartment became my fortress of solitude, my place to crumble without anyone watching. The moment I sat on that couch, it felt like the four walls were closing in on me. All I could think about was 2018 Carl, 2019 Carl—drink, coke, girls, party. The memories flooded back, and with them came the cravings.

In those first few weeks back in the city, I started isolating myself. Friends would call and invite me out, and I'd decline.

"I'm not interested. I'm just gonna chill tonight," I'd say. But "chill" had taken on a new meaning. It meant staying home, drinking by myself and doing cocaine by myself. It meant putting on music or watching TV in a desperate attempt to drown out the thoughts in my head.

And then, inevitably, after hours alone with those substances, I'd start making calls. I'd reach out to friends, family, my mom, anyone who might pick up at three in the morning. I'd ramble, sometimes crying hysterically, occasionally angry, rarely coherent. I was scaring people, calling at all hours of the night, and being emotionally volatile. But I could justify it all because I was grieving. I was the brother who had just lost his brother. Who could blame me for being a mess?

The cycle was persistent. Wake up feeling like shit, both physically and emotionally. Try to function through the day. Start drinking again as soon as it seemed acceptable, which, in my distorted reality, was getting earlier and earlier. Add cocaine to keep me going when the alcohol would have put me to sleep. Pass out, wake up, repeat.

My drinking and drug use wasn't just about numbing the pain of losing Curtis. It was also about avoiding the complicated feelings I had about our relationship. The regret of not meeting with him when I had the chance that summer. The guilt over how I'd spoken about his addiction on TV had created a rift between us. The shame of recognizing myself in his struggles, of seeing how similar our paths had been despite my best efforts to be different.

These emotions were too raw, too overwhelming to face sober. So, I didn't.

There's a particular moment that stands out in my memory from this period. It was Thanksgiving 2020. My cast member and I had decided to spend it together, just the two of us and a few close friends. We cooked, we set the table, we tried to create some semblance of normalcy in a year that had been anything but normal.

As the evening progressed, I started drinking whiskey—Jack Daniel's, specifically. Anyone who knows me can tell you that Jack turns me into a very aggressive, intense person. I become combative, looking to talk shit and pick fights. This night was no exception.

My cast member and I started bickering about the pot roast. Maybe it was in too long, and maybe it wasn't done right. All of the details are fuzzy now, but the emotion isn't. What began as a minor disagreement quickly escalated into something much bigger. I felt the familiar anger rising, the kind that alcohol always amplified. Before I knew it, I was shouting, "Fuck you, I'm done, I'm leaving!"

I walked out of the apartment—this was Thanksgiving dinner, mind you—went down ten floors to my place, closed the door, called my dealer, ordered another bottle, and sat there alone. Eventually, some friends from upstairs came down to check on me, and instead of helping me, they joined the party. We did more drugs together, and the night spiraled even further.

The next day, two cast members essentially told me that they couldn't be friends with me if I continued acting like this. But even their ultimatums weren't enough to shake me out of the path I was on. I was too far gone, too lost in grief and substances to hear them.

Christmas was much the same story. It was attempts at normalcy derailed by my drinking and drug use. New Year's Eve, a holiday I'd never spent at home in my entire adult life, found me alone in my apartment, too mentally and emotionally exhausted to face the world. I ignored calls and texts from concerned friends, unable to pick up the phone and pretend I was okay.

January 1, 2021, came and went, and I remained in my isolation, dodging attempts at connection, sinking deeper into a hole that seemed to have no bottom. I had hit a point where I was almost apathetic about living. Not actively suicidal, but indifferent to whether I woke up the next day. It was a dangerous place to be, especially with the amounts of alcohol and cocaine I was consuming.

Then came January 6, 2021—a date now infamous for the insurrection at the Capitol. I was working from home, like most people during the pandemic. It was a long day of Zoom calls and emails for Loverboy, stretching into the evening. As the day progressed, I began hearing about protests in D.C. They were intensifying. Trump had spoken, stirring up the crowd. CNN was on in the background as I worked, and I couldn't tear my eyes away from the unfolding pandemonium.

I'm gonna start drinking, fuck it, I thought. *That'll help me get through the rest of the work.* So, I opened a bottle of wine and drank it within about half an hour, all while trying to respond to emails and watch the news simultaneously. By eleven p.m., I'd shut my computer, finished the bottle, and was fully absorbed in the surreal scenes playing out on my TV.

The sight of rioters taking over the Capitol filled me with a mix of anger, confusion, and despair. It was infuriating, regardless of political stance and watching this happen in our country was deeply unsettling. In my increasingly intoxicated state, those emotions amplified.

That's when I made the call, the same call I'd made countless times before. I ordered cocaine, but this time, I went big. Three giant jars, a better deal to buy all at once. A quantity that would be enough for a football team.

Alone in my apartment, I went on a bender that lasted well into the morning. The news continued to get worse, showing videos of people inside the Capitol, and I kept drinking and doing more coke. By five a.m., I was pacing around my apartment, barely coherent but somehow remembering that I had a business call scheduled for later that morning with Nick at Loverboy.

At 6:30 a.m., I texted Nick to cancel. He knew me well enough by this point to sense when something was wrong. He called me instantly, and I could barely put words together. Concerned, he called Kyle, who then reached out to check on me.

During this time, I had also started texting an executive producer. My brother's episode was going to air in a couple months and the weight of that reality was crashing down on me. I was spiraling. I couldn't stop drinking or doing drugs. I was crumbling right before my own eyes. Honestly, I thought I was about to die. My body felt like it was shutting down.

I called the executive at eight a.m. on a weekday, utterly incoherent. I don't remember what I said or what he said, but I do know I hung up the phone.

Another mutual person called afterward, trying to talk me down, telling me to sleep it off. I finally passed out sometime that day and woke up later that night to a phone full of texts from concerned people at Bravo, from Kyle asking if I was alright, and from friends checking in.

That night, for the first time, I truly feared for my life. The anxiety I felt upon waking was unlike anything I'd experienced before. Looking at all those texts, seeing what I'd done, feeling like complete shit from all the drugs and alcohol. It scared the hell out of me. This wasn't just partying too hard anymore. This wasn't just having a wild night. I was completely destroying myself.

In that moment of clarity, I reached out to a friend who had gotten sober. Months earlier, he had called to tell me he was in recovery, and he had asked if I was going to AA. When I said no, he had warned me, "You're not going to stay sober." He knew me, knew how we partied together and learned the depths of my issues with alcohol and drugs. Now, in my darkest hour, he was the lifeline I grabbed for.

He immediately connected me with a sponsor, a guy who had over ten years of sobriety. This man worked at Goldman Sachs, one of the world's largest investment banks, and was incredibly successful. Yet he took the time to get on a call with me, a guy he'd never met, because that's what recovery communities do; they show up for each other.

On that call, he told me about his own addiction, how he'd struggled with cocaine and alcohol just like me. The similarities between our stories really hit me. Hearing this guy, who seemed to have his life together, describe the same destructive patterns I was stuck in was like looking in a mirror. For the first time, I could actually see myself clearly, and what I saw was fucking terrifying.

He told me we would talk every day for the next ninety days. He instructed me to download the *Alcoholics Anonymous Big Book* and the 12 Steps. He laid out a plan, a path forward through the darkness I'd been lost in. And for the first time in months, maybe years, I felt a glimmer of hope.

The next day, Kyle came to my apartment. He sat me down and had a brutal, honest conversation with me.

"Dude, you gotta stop," he said. "You're killing yourself." When Kyle said that, it really got to me. He'd been there for all of it—the nights out, the partying, watching me spiral. He knew me better than almost anyone, and he was actually scared I was going to die.

That conversation, combined with the wake-up call from the night before and connecting with a sponsor, finally did the trick. January seventh and eighth, 2021, were the days I looked at myself and said, *I have to change.* January eighth became my first day sober. That's the date that changed everything for me.

Looking back on the months between Curtis's death and that January rock bottom, I see now how grief and addiction fed each other in a vicious cycle. The pain of losing my brother drove me deeper into substance abuse, and the substances prevented me from healthily processing that grief. I was stuck in a loop, each day darker than the last.

I also see how Curtis's death brought into sharp focus the issues I'd been struggling with for years. My brother and I shared the same genes, the same predispositions to addiction, and the same demons. Watching him lose his battle with those demons was like seeing a possible future for myself, a future I was hurtling toward at full speed.

During those months before sobriety, I completely lost faith in myself. Before Curtis died, I'd been trying to cut back on drinking, actually making some progress in therapy, and being honest about my problems for the first time in my life. His death shattered that tentative progress, sending me back to square one, or rather, several squares behind where I'd started. I felt like a failure, as if I was dishonoring his memory by falling apart so completely.

But that's how addiction works. It gets worse when you hide it and feel like shit about it. The more you keep it secret, the more you lie about it, the stronger it gets. By pretending to be okay, by maintaining the charade that I was handling everything well, I was only feeding the beast that was consuming me from the inside out.

The months after Curtis's death were the lowest point of my life, but they were also, in a strange way, necessary. They showed me that there was no middle ground for me when it came to substances. Moderation was not an option. It was either complete sobriety or complete destruction. There was no in-between path I could walk.

Those months also connected me, however painfully, to my brother's experience. I began to understand on a deeper level what he had gone through, the battles he had fought, the demons he had wrestled with. I started to see his addiction not as a moral failing or a weakness but as a disease that he had struggled against with every fiber of his being. And in that understanding, I found a new kind of compassion, for him and, eventually, for myself.

In the depths of my grief and addiction, I had used Curtis's death as an excuse to self-destruct. "My brother just died" became my get-out-of-jail-free card for continued substance abuse. But in recovery, I began to use his memory differently and as motivation to stay sober, to be the brother he would be proud of, to carry on the work of helping others that had been so important to him in his final days.

But that realization didn't come immediately. First, I had to hit my own rock bottom and had to face the stark reality that if I continued on the path I was on, I would likely end up just like Curtis; another life lost to the cruel grip of addiction. I had to reach the point where the pain of staying the same finally outweighed the pain of change.

The day I couldn't hide anymore, not from others, and more importantly, not from myself. It was the day I finally admitted that I had a problem I couldn't solve on my own, that I needed help, that the path I was on led only to one destination, and it wasn't one I wanted to reach.

The months between August 2020 and January 2021 were the darkest of my life. They were filled with pain, self-destruction, and a grief so profound it felt like it would swallow me whole. But they were also the months that ultimately led me to sobriety, to a new understanding of myself and my brother, to a path of healing that, while difficult, has been more rewarding than I could have imagined.

Curtis's death was the catalyst for both my darkest months and my eventual recovery. In losing him, I nearly lost myself. But in finding sobriety, I found a way to honor him, to carry his memory forward, to turn the pain of his loss into purpose. It's not the journey either of us would have chosen, but it's the one that brought me to where I am today—sober, present, and determined to make each day count in a way that would make my brother proud.

That's the thing about rock bottom—once you hit it, the only way left to go is up. And on January 8, 2021, I finally started that upward climb.

Chapter 13

IT'S ONE THING TO decide to get sober. It's another thing entirely to stay that way.

My sponsor was transformative. He laid out a path forward, a structured approach to recovery that I desperately needed.

We would open up the 12 Steps, the Alcoholics Anonymous book. He would make me read it out loud over the phone to him. Then, he would read chapters. We would go back and forth, reading.

The first few days of sobriety were physically brutal. The withdrawals, the shakes, the insomnia, the racing thoughts. My body and mind rebelled against the absence of substances that had become as essential as air. But there was also a strange clarity emerging through the fog, moments of presence I hadn't experienced in years.

When I got sober, I had to face not just the damage I'd done to myself through substances but the unresolved trauma that had fueled so much of my addiction.

The early days of sobriety are like learning to walk again. Everything feels new, raw, and uncomfortable. Simple social interactions that I'd navigated with the buffer of alcohol for years suddenly seemed daunting. How do you make small talk without a drink in your hand? How do you deal with awkward silences or uncomfortable emotions without the escape hatch of intoxication?

My sponsor guided me through this unfamiliar terrain. We worked through the 12 Steps methodically and deliberately. I wrote down lists of people I needed to make amends to. My parents, people I'd dated, friends, and family members.

I conducted what is known as a "moral inventory," delving deeply into my life, patterns, and behaviors.

It's a painful exercise, but it's also essential. You stack these sessions with your sponsor when going to meetings.

I attended Zoom meetings in the morning, logging on to a group in New York but keeping my camera off. I was still scared to talk, to identify myself as an alcoholic. It was foreign territory, uncomfortable and exposing. But gradually, with my sponsor's guidance, I became more comfortable sharing and more willing to be vulnerable about my struggles.

One of the most challenging aspects of early sobriety is confronting all the emotions you've been numbing for years. They come flooding in without the chemical barrier you've relied on. And you have to sit with them, feel them, process them. There's no escape, no shortcut. It's fucking overwhelming because, for years, I'd trained myself to reach for a bottle or a line whenever things got uncomfortable—sad, angry, anxious, bored, whatever. Now, suddenly, I was feeling everything at full volume with no way to turn it down, and some days, the grief about Curtis would hit me out of nowhere, or I'd get irrationally angry about traffic because I had no idea how to process anything without numbing it. Learning that emotions don't actually kill you, even when they feel like they might, was one of the hardest lessons of early sobriety.

For me, this meant finally confronting the complicated feelings I had about Curtis, about his death, and about our relationship. It meant acknowledging the trauma I'd experienced and perpetuated. It meant taking responsibility for my actions rather than blaming others or circumstances.

I get on a phone call with my sponsor. Even at night, at eight or nine o'clock. He had two kids, he was married, and he had been sober for ten years, but he would take the time, sometimes up to an hour, and we would open up the 12 Steps.

Sobriety isn't just about not drinking or doing drugs. It's about addressing the root causes of why you turned to those substances in the first place. It's about developing new coping mechanisms and new ways of dealing with stress, anxiety, social pressure, and boredom. All the triggers that are used to send you reaching for a bottle or a bag.

I threw myself into activities that supported my sobriety. I underwent a lot of acupuncture, which helped with processing grief by calming my nervous system and giving me a space to just be still with my emotions. I went to therapy regularly. I meditated. I exercised. I established routines that gave structure to my days. Making my bed every morning, going for walks, and staying physically active are all habits that contribute to my overall well-being.

There's psychology around making your bed. It sounds silly, but it cultivates a mindset of order and self-care. When you're in early recovery, your brain is in a state of flux. You're dealing with chaos internally, so having something external that you can control, something that creates order in your physical space, actually helps calm your mind. It's like telling yourself, "I can handle this. I can take care of myself."

Making your bed is proof that you accomplished something before most people are even awake. It sets a tone for the day that you're someone who follows through and takes care of your space. And at the end of a shitty day, when everything went wrong, you still come home to a made bed. It's this small thing that says your day wasn't a complete loss. You did something right, even if it was just pulling the covers up and straightening the pillows.

But the real test came with social situations. How was I supposed to go to parties and events that had always revolved around drinking? It scared the shit out of me.

Social events are all about people loosening up, letting their guards down, and connecting through shared inhibition. Alcohol had always been my social lubricant, my liquid courage, my permission slip to be louder, more outgoing, more engaging. Without it, I worried I would be boring, awkward, and sidelined.

But I was committed to my sobriety. I had to find a way to be myself without the substances I'd relied on for so long. I had to relearn how to socialize, how to handle conflicts, and how to navigate intense dynamics, all while in recovery.

Mocktails and non-alcoholic beers were my best friends. That's when I really started trying to figure out what I could drink, and I began to learn that I just needed something in my hands. They gave me something to hold, something to sip on during social situations, eliminating the awkward "Why aren't you drinking?" questions.

The first social event was surreal. Everyone else was drinking and partying as usual while I was experiencing it all through a new, crystal-clear lens. I observed behaviors, dynamics, and patterns that I'd been too drunk to notice before. I saw how alcohol transformed people, how it fueled arguments, and how it created conflicts that seemed significant in the moment but meaningless in the light of day. People would get into screaming matches over nothing, a drama that felt earth-shattering at two a.m. but was forgotten entirely by noon. I watched friends turn into different versions of themselves after a few drinks, saying shit they'd never say sober, then acting surprised when they had to deal with the mess they'd made.

And I noticed something unexpected: I didn't miss it. Yes, there were moments of social awkwardness, moments when I felt slightly out of sync with the group's energy. However, there were also moments of genuine connection, authentic conversation, and being fully present in a way I hadn't been for years.

After a couple of gatherings, I would wake up feeling great while everybody else was hungover and tired. I was energetic, feeling good, and had my wits about me. I quickly realized that I wished I had done this sooner, as I was actually having a better experience.

Having a regular job presented its own challenges. How do you navigate work culture when everything revolves around happy hours and networking events with drinking? How do you attend industry functions and maintain connections while staying sober? It was fucking hard at first, trying to figure out how to be the same person professionally without my usual social crutch.

During the pandemic, when everything was remote, it was manageable. I could work from home and handle my responsibilities without the face-to-face aspects that involved drinking. But as restrictions lifted and in-person events resumed,

I had to find a way to navigate professional settings without compromising my sobriety.

It gave me a structure. By structure, I mean I woke up every morning, and I had accountability. I had to be awake. I had emails to respond to. I had phone calls. I had a particular obligation because I was an employee.

One of the most significant changes in sobriety was how I thought about Curtis. When I was using, I'd used his death as an excuse to keep spiraling, like a free pass to destroy myself even more. In sobriety, I started seeing him differently—as a warning, as motivation, as something guiding me toward a better path.

I started to understand on a deeper level what he had gone through, the battles he had fought, and the anxieties he had wrestled with.

I started seeing him not just as my brother but as my higher power, my guiding light. I'm not super religious, but I found this deep connection to him, using his memory to protect me and push me to be better. When I'd get tempted to drink or do something stupid, I'd think about Curtis and what he'd want for me.

The mental health aspects of recovery can't be overstated. Getting sober doesn't automatically fix your mental health issues. In many ways, it brings them into sharper focus. Without substances to blur the edges to provide temporary relief, you have to face your depression, anxiety, trauma, and insecurities head-on.

For me, this meant addressing the deep-seated self-doubts that had followed me from childhood. Being bullied for my appearance, feeling like I never quite fit in, and always trying to prove myself. It meant confronting the shame and guilt I carried about my past behavior, the relationships I'd damaged, and the opportunities I'd squandered.

It was also my first time doing therapy where I was telling the one hundred percent truth. I'd done therapy in the six years previous, but I never once, up until January 2024, said, "I drink a ton. I've done drugs. I've partied." And it was liberating to actually open up with a therapist who focuses on alcohol issues and be completely honest.

That honesty was transformative. For years, I'd compartmentalized, minimized, and lied to myself and others about the severity of my issues. I'd blamed relationships, work stress, and anything but the real problem: me and my choices.

I was blaming others in relationships. I was blaming external factors except for myself. After a while, you start pointing fingers. I started losing friends. People did not want to hang out with me because I was a lot to be around.

In sobriety, I had to take responsibility for my actions, for my patterns, for my part in the chaos that had characterized so much of my life. I had to acknowledge that while external factors, grief, pressure, and trauma had contributed to my addiction, ultimately, the choice was mine alone.

This kind of radical honesty is uncomfortable and even painful. But it's also liberating. There's a freedom in facing yourself fully, in dropping the pretenses that addiction requires. There's relief in not having to keep track of lies, in not having to maintain an increasingly complex facade.

As I progressed in my sobriety, I began to discover aspects of myself that had been buried under years of substance abuse. I rediscovered interests and passions that had been set aside. I developed a deeper appreciation for simple pleasures: a good conversation, a beautiful day, a moment of connection.

I also found myself becoming more grounded, more present, and more capable of dealing with life's challenges without immediately seeking escape. Problems that would have sent me into a panic before became manageable growth opportunities rather than excuses for self-destruction.

I felt like I looked the best I've looked in a while. I was healthy.

Physical health is intertwined with mental health, and sobriety brought improvements on both fronts. My skin cleared up, I lost the puffiness that had previously characterized my face, and I started working out more consistently. I slept better, had more energy, and felt more alive in my own body.

These physical changes were visible to others. Friends commented on how good I looked, something that boosted my confidence during a vulnerable time. The external validation was nice, but the internal changes were more significant.

I was starting to like myself again, to respect myself, to see potential rather than just past failures.

Of course, recovery isn't linear. There were setbacks, difficult days, and moments of doubt. There were times when the thought of a drink was so tempting that it took every ounce of willpower to resist. There were social situations I avoided entirely because I wasn't sure I could navigate them sober. Some relationships changed, some for the better, some not.

One of the principles of recovery is "one day at a time." It's cliché, but it's also profoundly true. Thinking about never drinking again for the rest of your life is overwhelming. But thinking about not drinking today, just for these twenty-four hours, that's manageable. And so you stack those days, building a foundation of sobriety day by day.

These little blocks, these little movements and actions each day that you make, compound on themselves.

The one-year mark in sobriety is a significant milestone. You've made it through a full year of everything: holidays, birthdays, anniversaries, all the shit that used to trigger you. It's proof you can handle anything without drinking or using. Many people never make it that far.

As I approached that anniversary, I felt a mix of pride, gratitude, and humility. Pride in what I'd accomplished, gratitude for the support that had made it possible, humility in the face of how much I still had to learn, how much work was still ahead.

The one-year rule in AA, the recommendation to avoid dating in your first year of sobriety, exists for a reason. Early recovery is a vulnerable, volatile, and consuming period. Adding the emotional intensity of a new relationship to that mix can be destabilizing, distracting from the essential work of building a solid foundation in sobriety.

The one-year thing doesn't make sense at first. But it's so apparent to me because I've experienced it firsthand. After six months, you think you can do it, but you still have more work to do. You need to get in touch with your voice, your opinion, and your own sense of self, and clearly define what that sense of self is so you can then show up authentically.

I understood the wisdom in this recommendation, even as I struggled with loneliness, the desire for connection, and the natural human yearning for companionship. Sobriety can be isolating, especially in a culture so centered around drinking. Dating provided a reprieve from that isolation, a sense of normalcy, and a feeling of moving forward with life rather than just recovering from it.

What I've learned in this process is that sobriety isn't solely about willpower. It's about connection to yourself, to others, to something larger than yourself. It's about finding purpose, meaning, and fulfillment that makes the temporary escape of substances seem hollow in comparison.

For me, that connection came through my relationship with Curtis's memory, through my daily work routines, through the authentic friendships I developed in recovery, and through the simple daily practices that grounded me in the present rather than pushing me to escape it.

The work of recovery never stops. It's constantly changing, always responding to new shit that comes up, new triggers, new things you learn about yourself. It's not just about not drinking or using drugs—it's about living honestly, being real, and facing whatever life throws at you without running away to get drunk.

That commitment isn't always easy to maintain. There are days when it feels like an uphill battle, especially when old patterns of thinking are loud, and the desire for escape is strong. But there are also days when it feels like the most natural thing in the world, when the clarity, presence, and authentic connection that sobriety enables seem worth any sacrifice.

That's the paradox of sobriety. What seems like restriction is actually freedom. Freedom from the cycle of addiction, from the shame of behavior you can't control, from the disconnection from yourself and others that substances create. Freedom to choose, to grow, to connect, to live with intention rather than impulse.

This freedom doesn't come easily or automatically. It's earned through consistent effort, difficult self-examination, and the humble admission that you need help, followed by the courageous decision to accept it. It's built day by day, choice by choice, one moment of presence at a time.

But it's worth it. Worth the discomfort of early sobriety, the challenging emotional work, the social awkwardness, and the fundamental reorientation of your life around recovery rather than escape. Worth it because what you gain, authenticity, connection, integrity, and presence, is so much more valuable than what you give up.

The real work begins when you put down the drink, the drug, the escape mechanism of choice. But it doesn't end there. It continues, day by day, choice by choice, as you build a life that supports your sobriety rather than threatens it, a self that embraces reality rather than fleeing from it, a future that holds promise rather than just more of the same destructive cycle.

That's what I started in January 2021. Not just quitting drinking but actually living. Not just avoiding the bad shit, but building something good. Not just dealing with my past but creating a future worth having. It's still going on today—the ups and downs, the things I learn about myself, the times I screw up, and the times I get it right. The real work of staying sober, being honest, and taking it one day at a time.

Chapter 14

THE HAMPTONS IN SUMMER is basically one giant party. Hot people, booze everywhere, staying up until sunrise, going from the beach straight to some club. It's everything I'd been staying away from since getting sober. And here I was, about to jump right back into that world, without drinking, with cameras following me around.

As I packed my bags for the summer house, a wave of anxiety washed over me. Six months sober and heading into the lion's den. The place where, for five summers running, I'd been the life of the party—the guy with a drink always in hand, the one suggesting another round, the one who'd keep the night going until sunrise. Who would I be there now?

My sponsor had concerns. "Are you sure this is the right environment for you right now?" he asked during one of our calls. It was a fair question. Recovery literature warns about putting yourself in high-risk situations, especially in early sobriety. And a summer house filled with alcohol, where drinking was central to the experience? That checked every box on the "maybe avoid this" list.

But I had made commitments. I had friendships there. And if I'm being honest, I needed to prove to myself that I could do it—that sobriety didn't mean the end of my social life, that I could still be Carl without the alcohol.

The drive out to the Hamptons that first weekend was surreal. I had spent so many Friday afternoons making that same drive, already buzzed from pregaming, excited for the debauchery ahead. This time, I packed cases of sparkling water and non-alcoholic beers. I had a plan for how I'd handle offers of drinks, questions about my sobriety, and the inevitable pressure to "just have one."

Walking into the house that first day was like entering a familiar place but with new eyes. The kitchen counter already displayed an impressive array of alcohol—wine bottles, liquor, seltzers, and beer. The gang was excited, already pouring drinks and planning the weekend's parties. For a second, I felt that old familiar pull—the house, the friends, the atmosphere all triggering that voice that whispers, "You can have just one."

But I had six months of sobriety tools under my belt. I unpacked my room and set up my little sobriety corner with my journal, meditation books, and the coin my sponsor had given me to mark my milestone. Then I headed to the kitchen and made myself a mocktail in a proper glass—something that looked like what everyone else was drinking but wouldn't compromise my sobriety.

The first night was the hardest. Everyone fell back into our old patterns except me. The drinks flowed, voices got louder, behavior got looser, and I watched it all happen with stone-cold clarity. I nursed my club soda with lime, laughing along and participating in conversations, but feeling as though I was watching the scene unfold from behind a glass.

Kyle noticed first. He pulled me aside around midnight. "You good, man?" he asked. The genuine concern in his voice touched me. He'd seen me at my lowest and had that heart-to-heart with me after my rock bottom. He knew better than most how significant this challenge was.

"It's weird," I admitted. "But I'm good. Really good, actually."

And I meant it. Once the initial awkwardness passed, I began to notice things. Like how conversations became repetitive after a certain number of drinks. How some conflicts escalated over nothing. How the energy in the room shifted as the night progressed—not always for the better.

The most remarkable difference came the next morning. I woke up at 7:30 a.m., clear-headed and rested. I made coffee and took it out to the deck, watching the sunrise over the trees. The house was completely silent—everyone else was still asleep, nursing what would be impressive hangovers when they finally emerged hours later.

I used those morning hours as my sanctuary throughout the summer. I'd work out, meditate, journal, and make breakfast. By the time others staggered downstairs, I'd already lived half a day. It gave me a strange sense of power, this ability to maximize time that was previously lost to recovery from the night before.

The toughest moments came during the day parties. In the Hamptons, day drinking is an art form. Brunches turn into day clubs turn into sunset gatherings. Everyone expected me to be the same party animal I'd always been. People were waiting for me to show up with a drink in hand, ready to get wild like every other summer.

I still went to these events, but with a different approach. I'd arrive later, leave earlier, and always have my exit strategy planned. I learned to be flexible—if a situation started feeling too triggering, I gave myself permission to leave without explanation. I kept a car available or knew which friends could give me a ride, so I was never stuck somewhere I couldn't handle.

About three weekends in, something unexpected happened. I was sitting at a day party at a beach club, sober among the chaos, when a friend of a friend sat down next to me.

"You're not drinking," she said. It wasn't a question.

"No," I replied, bracing for the usual follow-up questions or pressure.

"Me neither. Six months next week." She raised her seltzer in a toast.

We spent the next hour talking about recovery while the party raged around us. She shared her story, and I shared mine. We exchanged numbers and promised to text each other if either of us needed support at any point in the summer. I realized I wasn't as alone as I'd thought, even in this environment. Sober people were everywhere. You just don't notice them when you were drinking.

After that, I started connecting with the sober community in the Hamptons. I found meetings I could attend between filming. I discovered restaurants with great mocktail menus. I built a parallel social life that supported my sobriety while still allowing me to maintain my existing friendships and commitments.

The dynamic in the house shifted as well. At first, my sobriety made some people uncomfortable—it held a mirror up to their own drinking in ways they weren't prepared to examine. But as the summer progressed, I became a sort of safe harbor for housemates having rough nights. The person who would ensure you got home safely. The one who remembered conversations. The one who could drive at two a.m. if needed.

Not drinking revealed which friendships were based primarily on partying and which had deeper, more lasting foundations. Some relationships strengthened during my sobriety. Others faded, and I had to come to terms with that loss. It wasn't always easy watching certain friendships drift because we no longer shared that central activity, but it created space for new, more authentic connections.

Dating was its own challenge. In previous summers, I'd relied on liquid courage for hookups and flirtations. Now, I had to navigate attraction and rejection with full awareness, with no buffer to dull the awkwardness or disappointment. I had some painfully awkward moments. I had to learn how to be charming, confident, and authentic without the crutch of alcohol—skills I'd never fully developed in my drinking years.

But there were unexpected benefits too. When I did connect with someone, the connection was real, not clouded by substances or likely to be forgotten in the morning. I started having conversations that went deeper than the surface-level small talk that dominated Hampton's social circles. I began to value the quality of interaction over quantity.

The cameras added another layer of complexity. In past seasons, alcohol had helped me ignore their presence and made me less self-conscious about being filmed during vulnerable or wild moments. Sober, I was acutely aware of being recorded, which created a strange kind of performance anxiety at first.

However, as the weeks passed, I developed a deeper understanding of the filming process. Instead of using alcohol to manufacture moments, I allowed myself to be more authentically present. The cameras captured a different side of me—more thoughtful, more measured, but also more genuine. I had conversations that I actually remembered the next day. I made decisions I didn't immediately regret when watching the footage later.

Halfway through the summer, we had a particularly big party at the house. Everyone was drinking heavily, the energy was chaotic, and I suddenly felt overwhelmed. I slipped out to the pool area, needing a moment of quiet. I sat at the edge of the water, feet dangling in, breathing deeply the way my therapist had taught me anxiety management.

A few minutes later, I heard the sliding door open. Amanda came out and sat beside me.

"Too much in there?" she asked.

I nodded. "Just needed some air."

"I've been watching you this summer," she said after a moment. "You seem ... I don't know. More yourself somehow."

Her observation hit me right in the heart. More myself. That was precisely it. Without alcohol blurring my edges, numbing my feelings, and altering my behavior, I was finally showing up as the actual Carl. Not the party persona I'd cultivated for years, not the character I thought people wanted, just me—with all my flaws, insecurities, strengths, and genuine qualities.

"Thanks," I said simply.

As the summer progressed, I developed rituals that helped maintain my sobriety. I'd wake up early for beach walks. I'd step outside during intense party moments to call my sponsor or another sober friend. I kept a journal of triggers and how I handled them. I started noticing the good stuff—getting through a wedding sober, having a complicated conversation without needing a drink, and actually enjoying things I'd only done drunk before.

The weeknight dinners were the best part of the week. Smaller groups, with less drinking, and just cooking together and actually talking to each other. I found myself looking forward to these quieter moments more than the big weekend blowouts. I started inviting friends over on the off nights, building a different kind of social life centered around quality time rather than partying.

Not every moment was easy. There were nights I lay awake, listening to the ongoing party downstairs, fighting the urge to join in "just this once." There were social events where I felt awkward, out of place, and unsure of how to navigate without the social lubricant of alcohol. Some conflicts were harder to brush off without the numbing effect of substances.

But for every difficult moment, there was a corresponding benefit. The mental clarity. Emotional stability. The physical health improvements. The authentic connections. The memories—actually remembering every conversation, every beautiful sunset, every meaningful interaction.

By August, I had settled into a rhythm. I knew which events I could handle and which to steer clear of. I had a solid routine that supported my sobriety even in this challenging environment. I'd built a reputation as the reliable one, the clear-headed one, which came with its own kind of social capital.

Labor Day weekend marked the traditional end of our summer season. As we prepared for one final blowout party, I found myself reflective rather than anxious. I'd made it through an entire summer—the most triggering season in the most triggering environment—completely sober. The accomplishment felt monumental.

The last night, as music pumped through the house and drinks flowed freely, I stepped outside to look at the stars. Kyle joined me, Loverboy in hand. There was genuine pride in his expression as he looked at me, and I could tell he'd been worried about me coming out here this summer. I'd been worried too.

But I had made it through. I was still fun, just without the mayhem that used to come with it. We stood in comfortable silence for a moment, looking at the night sky.

As we watched the stars, I realized something that had surprised me throughout the summer. Staying sober hadn't been the hardest part. The hardest part had been figuring out who I was without drinking, discovering who Carl was when he was just Carl, no additives.

As I packed up my room on that final Monday, I looked around the house that had seen so many of my highest and lowest moments over the years. I'd entered this summer with trepidation, worried that sobriety would make me an outsider in a place that had been central to my identity. Instead, I discovered that I could still belong here but on different, healthier terms.

The drive back to the city felt symbolic. I was leaving behind not just another summer but the old version of myself that had dominated those Hamptons seasons for years. The party boy, the wild one, the guy who needed substances to feel confident or connected. In his place was someone more grounded, more authentic, more aware.

As I hit the highway, I reflected on what I'd accomplished. I had made it through. The feeling that washed over me was one I could only describe as freedom. Not the freedom to drink whenever I wanted, but the freedom from needing to. The freedom to be myself without chemical assistance. The freedom to remember every moment, good and bad, and learn from it all.

As the Hamptons faded in my rearview mirror, I felt a deep sense of accomplishment. I had faced one of my biggest challenges in early sobriety and emerged stronger for it. The summer, once the epicenter of my drinking life, had become part of my recovery story instead.

The road ahead still held plenty of challenges. But if I could navigate a summer in the Hamptons while maintaining my sobriety, I could handle whatever came next. One day at a time, as we say in recovery. One moment, one choice, one authentic interaction at a time.

And for the first time in years, I was looking forward to all of it; clear-eyed, present, and genuinely myself.

Chapter 15

THE IRONY WASN'T LOST on me: a newly sober guy working for an alcohol company. If someone had pitched this as a storyline, I'd have laughed it off as too on-the-nose. But that was exactly where I found myself after getting sober, promoting a product I could no longer consume.

Working at Loverboy had been an exciting venture before sobriety. I'd joined my friend Kyle's company with enthusiasm, believing in the brand, enjoying the perks, and feeling like I was building something meaningful. When I made the decision to get sober, one of my immediate concerns was what it would mean for my role at the company. How do you represent a beverage you can't drink? How do you sell something that nearly destroyed your life?

During the pandemic, this contradiction was manageable. Most of our work was remote: Zoom calls, marketing planning, distributor relationships. All could be handled from behind a screen. I wasn't faced with the daily temptation of product sampling or customer events. I could separate my professional identity from my personal recovery.

However, when everything started reopening, that's when it got really hard. Suddenly, I had to go to launch parties, distributor meetings, and marketing events, all revolving around alcohol. I had to figure out how to do my job without drinking, which was way more complex than it sounds.

My first in-person event after getting sober was scary. I remember standing in a crowded bar, surrounded by people drinking Loverboy products, holding my Red Bull in a regular glass to avoid the inevitable questions. Every fiber of my being felt the dissonance of the situation. I was the face of a brand I couldn't safely consume. The cognitive disconnect was jarring.

I developed strategies, of course. I became an expert at the "fake sip" for photos. I learned to deflect questions about my favorite flavor with humor or by turning the question back on the asker. I became proficient at describing taste profiles from memory rather than experience. I could talk about the "light, refreshing citrus notes" of a product I hadn't tasted in months.

The reality was that working for Loverboy while sober was like walking a tightrope without a net. On one side, there was my commitment to sobriety: the promise I'd made to myself after hitting rock bottom. On the other hand, there was my responsibility to the company, to Kyle, and to our team. Finding a balance between these competing forces became a daily practice.

What made it possible during that time was the structure. In early sobriety, having a job (any job) was crucial. It gave me accountability, routine, and purpose. Loverboy provided that framework when I desperately needed it. I woke up every morning with emails to answer, calls to make, and objectives to meet. When your internal world feels chaotic, having external order can be a lifeline. The job became a stabilizing force in my early recovery storm.

There were also moments of unexpected growth. Sobriety sharpened my business acumen. Without the fog of substances, I could see opportunities more clearly, think more strategically, and communicate more effectively. The same clarity that made social situations more challenging made professional situations more navigable.

The most difficult aspects were the industry events. Picture this: hundreds of people sampling our products, the energy high, music pumping, everyone gradually getting looser as the night progresses, and me, not drinking, trying to maintain the enthusiasm and energy expected of a brand representative. These events were marathons of endurance, testing my commitment hour by hour.

I'd attend with my Red Bull or water, standing amidst drunk fans wanting photos, trying to maintain the energy and enthusiasm without the boost that everyone else was enjoying from our products. It was exhausting but also rewarding. Proof that I could do my job, be entertaining, and connect with people, all without the use of substances.

There were awkward moments, of course. The inevitable "Why aren't you drinking your own product?" question came up regularly. Early on, I fumbled these interactions, providing vague answers such as "taking a break" or "driving tonight." As I became more secure in my sobriety, I found ways to be more honest without making others uncomfortable. "I don't drink anymore, but I'd love to hear what you think of it," became my standard response.

The reactions were interesting. Some people immediately became uncomfortable, some were overly supportive in that slightly patronizing way, and some just nodded and moved on. What I learned is that most people care far less about your drinking habits than you think they do. Their focus is on their experience, not your choices.

Working in the alcohol industry while sober gave me a unique perspective on drinking culture. I watched as social events transformed throughout the night: how the first drink made people more relaxed, the second more talkative, the third more uninhibited, and then the gradual slide into behavior people might regret the next day. I saw the business side of creating products designed to lower inhibitions, evoke specific feelings, and facilitate certain social experiences.

This perspective was sometimes uncomfortable. There were moments I felt like I was on the wrong side of the equation, promoting something that I knew firsthand could be destructive. But I also saw the other side: most people enjoyed our products responsibly, using them as part of celebrations or relaxed social gatherings and never crossing into the territory that had been so dangerous for me.

The truth about the alcohol industry is that it's not inherently evil, just as alcohol itself isn't inherently dangerous for everyone. My problem with alcohol was *my* problem: a complex interaction of genetics, psychology, trauma, and choices. That realization helped me reconcile my role at Loverboy with my personal recovery for a time.

Kyle was supportive throughout this transition. Our friendship had evolved through my sobriety. He'd seen me at my worst and had been instrumental in my decision to get help. Having a boss who understood my journey made the professional complexity more manageable. We never directly addressed the elephant in the room (that I was selling a product that had nearly killed me), but there was an unspoken understanding, a respect for the boundaries I needed to maintain.

What surprised me most was how my sobriety became an asset in certain contexts. In an industry where everyone is drinking, the sober guy remembers every conversation, follows up on every lead, and notices details that others miss. While everyone else was nursing hangovers the morning after events, I was clear-headed, productive, and ready to capitalize on the connections made the night before.

There's a strange duality to promoting a product you don't use: you become both insider and outsider simultaneously. You know all the internal language, the marketing angles, the brand positioning, but you're viewing it through a different lens than your customers. This perspective allowed me to see both the appeal of what we were selling and the reality of what it delivered.

I learned to separate the product from my experience with it. Loverboy wasn't the problem. My relationship with alcohol was the problem. For many people, our products were just pleasant beverages enjoyed in moderation, part of balanced social lives. My inability to moderate didn't mean the product itself was harmful to everyone.

This realization was liberating for a while. It allowed me to promote the brand with authenticity, not pretending I still drank, but acknowledging that for many people, our products enhanced their experiences rather than derailing their lives. I could stand behind the quality, the craftsmanship, and the brand values without endorsing the excessive consumption that had been my downfall.

There were still moments of temptation, especially on hard days when stress mounted or after difficult interactions when I remembered how alcohol temporarily numbed uncomfortable feelings. The accessibility made these moments more challenging; the product was literally everywhere in my professional life. But each time I navigated these situations without drinking, my resolve strengthened.

The question I got asked most frequently was whether working around alcohol made staying sober harder. The surprising answer is: not really. Physical proximity to alcohol wasn't my primary trigger. My triggers were more emotional: stress, anxiety, social discomfort, boredom. Being around alcohol professionally actually helped demystify it and strip away its allure. When you see something as a product (with marketing strategies, profit margins, supply chain challenges), it loses some of its emotional power over you.

What made it difficult were the spaces where alcohol was consumed. Bars, clubs, large parties. These environments were designed for a different kind of interaction than what I was capable of sober. The loud music that's tolerable when tipsy is overwhelming when sober. All those conversations that seemed so deep when everyone was wasted turned out to be completely meaningless when I was sober. It was hard to deal with, but it also made me certain that I was doing the right thing by staying clean.

Over time, however, the fundamental contradiction of my position became increasingly difficult to ignore. It doesn't make much sense to work somewhere that's constantly promoting something you can't be around. As my recovery progressed and I gained more clarity about the kind of life I wanted to build, I began to question whether Loverboy was still the right place for me.

Leaving wasn't easy. Kyle wasn't just my boss; he was my friend, and we'd built something real together. I loved the structure and purpose the job gave me when I was barely holding it together. But I knew that staying sober meant making choices that actually fit with who I was becoming, even when they hurt.

When I finally talked to Kyle about stepping back, it was one of the hardest conversations I've ever had. I was scared I'd mess up our friendship, let the whole team down, and walk away from something we'd built together. But Kyle completely understood and supported me, which honestly surprised me. He understood way better than I thought he would. He saw that trying to stay sober while selling alcohol wasn't something I could just tough out forever.

Leaving Loverboy was part of a larger process of reevaluating what I wanted my life to look like in sobriety. The job helped me when I needed it most, giving me stability when everything else in my life was falling apart. But as I got stronger in my recovery, I realized I needed work that didn't constantly conflict with who I was trying to become.

For months after leaving, I focused on other projects and continued building my recovery foundation. I explored various career paths and considered what kind of work would align better with my new lifestyle and values.

Then came the call I wasn't expecting. Kyle wanted to meet for coffee to discuss a new direction for Loverboy: a non-alcoholic line that the company was developing. The market for premium non-alcoholic beverages was growing rapidly, and Kyle saw both a business opportunity and a chance to expand the brand in a direction that could appeal to everyone, including both drinkers and non-drinkers.

Kyle wanted me involved in this project. Not just because I'd be the perfect person to help develop and market a non-alcoholic line, but because he missed working with me. This time, though, it would be different.

The proposal was intriguing: I would return as a consultant, focused explicitly on the non-alcoholic line, with the flexibility to pursue other projects and interests simultaneously. Rather than being embedded in the alcohol side of the business, I would be helping build something new, something that actually aligned with my sober lifestyle.

It felt like the universe offering a surprising resolution to a contradiction I'd thought was irreconcilable. I could stay connected to a brand and team I actually cared about, use my business skills, and do it in a way that helped my sobriety instead of threatening it. The flexibility allowed me to continue exploring other things and maintain the balanced life I was finally building.

After careful consideration and discussions with my sponsor and trusted friends, I decided to accept the offer. Returning to Loverboy in this new capacity felt right, not a step backward but a different path forward, one that honored both my history with the company and the new life I was creating.

Working on the non-alcoholic line gave me a new sense of purpose. I could bring my personal experience into product development conversations in a way that hadn't been possible before. "This tastes too artificial," I might say, or "The mouthfeel isn't gratifying enough to replace a cocktail." My sobriety, which had once been an awkward contradiction in my role, became a valuable asset.

There was something deeply satisfying about helping create products that allowed people to participate in social situations without alcohol, the very thing I had struggled with in early sobriety. Every time we got positive feedback from a sober customer who felt included rather than sidelined at social gatherings because of our products, a sense of purpose enveloped me that transcended business metrics.

The greatest lesson from my journey with Loverboy was that life rarely offers clean, simple solutions to complex situations. Sometimes, the path forward requires a detour, a period of separation, before a new and better configuration becomes possible. Recovery doesn't happen in isolation. It happens while continuing to live in the world with all its messy complications and contradictions. Sometimes, the path forward isn't about removing all potential triggers; it's about learning to navigate them with new awareness and different tools. And sometimes, it's about transforming a situation that once created conflict into one that supports growth.

In recovery circles, there's often talk about "living amends": the daily practice of living differently as a form of making things right. Working at Loverboy while maintaining my sobriety became a kind of living amends to myself, a daily recommitment to the path I'd chosen, regardless of the circumstances around me. Leaving was another form of that commitment, choosing alignment over contradiction, authenticity over compromise. And returning for the non-alcoholic line became yet another expression of the same principle: finding ways to contribute positively while honoring my recovery journey.

I'm grateful for my entire experience with Loverboy, from the early challenges to the difficult decision to leave to the unexpected opportunity to return in a new capacity. Each part of that whole experience taught me something about myself, about business, about how to handle complicated situations without compromising who I was becoming. Being sober in a world that revolved around drinking, knowing when to step back, and figuring out a new way to do my job changed my recovery in ways I never saw coming. It forced me to develop stronger boundaries, more transparent communication, and a more nuanced understanding of my relationship with work and identity.

Recovery isn't a straight line but a series of decisions, large and small, about the kind of life you want to build and the person you want to become. My journey with Loverboy (through all its phases) has been an integral part of that process, teaching me valuable lessons about what it means to live soberly, not just in the technical sense of abstaining from substances but in the deeper sense of living with awareness, intention, and authenticity.

Chapter 16

EVERYONE IN RECOVERY KNOWS the rules about dating in your first year. It's not just a suggestion; it's practically a commandment. There's wisdom in it that I understand now in ways I couldn't when I first heard it. When you're new in recovery, you're becoming a different person. You're learning to feel emotions without numbing them, to navigate social situations without relying on liquid courage, and to sit with discomfort instead of drowning in it. Adding the intensity of a romantic relationship to that volatile mix is like throwing a match into a room full of gas fumes.

But knowing something intellectually and living by it are two very different things.

At around seven months sober, I found myself drawn to someone in ways that surprised me. Lindsay Hubbard and I had been friends for years, but during that summer, we spent a lot of time together, not at wild parties or in chaotic group settings, but in quiet moments. We'd cook dinner together during the week. We'd hang out and watch TV. Simple, everyday activities that most people take for granted, but which I was now experiencing with new clarity.

When you build a bond with someone while sober, you develop more genuine emotions and feelings. Our friendship was deepening, becoming something more intimate. Lindsay and I could talk about anything. We supported each other through difficult moments. We were spending more and more time together, and I found myself looking forward to that time together.

But I was torn. On one side, there was this growing attraction and connection. On the other hand, there was the voice of my sponsor, the wisdom of AA literature, and the "one-year rule" that I'd heard repeatedly in meetings. I was still attending Zoom meetings every morning, still working through the steps, and still very much focused on building my foundation in sobriety.

It created this strange internal conflict. How do you reconcile these opposing forces? Am I supposed to ignore my feelings for someone I genuinely care about because of a rule in a book that's a hundred years old? But then again, that book and those rules had saved my life. Who was I to think I knew better?

The reality is that recovery takes a different form for everyone. Nobody gets sober and immediately goes on a reality TV show. That's not normal. Most people who hit rock bottom get a year of sobriety in treatment centers or live quietly, gradually rebuilding their lives. They don't get thrown into social environments that are literally designed for drama and spectacle. My situation was different, and I had to figure my own way through it.

What made things even more complicated was that the feelings seemed mutual. After officiating Kyle and Amanda's wedding, I had an honest conversation where I explained that I was taking things one day at a time and that I wasn't ready to date because of where I was in my sobriety. It was one of the hardest conversations I'd ever had: being completely transparent about my recovery needs while also acknowledging my genuine feelings.

But a week later, after a concert in New York City, I found myself having a heart-to-heart conversation with Lindsay that changed everything. The question of a future together hit me in a place of deep vulnerability. I could see that future. But I was scared. I was nervous. I was still figuring out who sober Carl really was.

At that moment, I decided to follow my heart. We became a couple that night, and with that decision, I entered a completely new territory: a sober relationship.

Dating while in recovery was unlike anything I'd experienced before. Most relationships follow a predictable pattern: you meet someone, you go for drinks, you loosen up with alcohol, and gradually get to know each other with that social lubricant always present. But we were building something different. From the flirting to the hand-holding to the deeper emotional connections, it was all happening in complete sobriety.

The early days of our relationship were marked by a unique intensity. Without the buffer of substances, every emotion was vivid, every interaction significant. I felt things more deeply than I had in previous relationships, both the positives and the negatives. When things were good between us, they were euphoric. When conflicts arose, they were overwhelming.

In some ways, dating before I'd reached my one-year sobriety mark complicated my recovery. The traditional wisdom about waiting a year exists for good reasons. When you're new in recovery, you need to focus entirely on building your relationship with yourself, on finding your voice, and on establishing your identity without substances. Introducing another person, especially in the intimate context of a romantic relationship, can distract from that essential work.

I can see that now, looking back. There were moments when the relationship became all-consuming when I directed energy toward my partner that might have been better spent on solidifying my own foundation. But there were also ways in which having support strengthened my commitment to sobriety. Having someone witness my transformation, celebrate my milestones, and stand by me during difficult moments mattered.

Love in sobriety had a clarity that I'd never experienced in my drinking days. I wasn't confusing lust with love. I wasn't making decisions in the fog of intoxication. I was present for every moment, every conversation, every realization about our compatibility and differences. I knew this person in ways I'd never known previous partners because I was actually there, fully engaged, not partially checked out in a haze of substances.

As our relationship progressed, I began to understand that sobriety isn't just about not drinking. It's about living honestly, facing life without escape mechanisms, and making choices when you're fully aware of what they mean. I tried to bring those same principles into the relationship. I wanted to communicate openly, deal with problems head-on instead of avoiding them, and be vulnerable about what scared me and what I hoped for.

However, relationships are complex, and no matter how well-intentioned one may be, no amount of effort can eliminate all challenges. Being with someone who still drank came with challenges. I had to adjust to social settings where alcohol was present and notice differences in how we experienced those nights. But she was also the person who supported me through milestones. Sometimes, this difference in perception led to disagreements about what had actually happened in certain situations.

There were moments of absolute joy, too. I remember waking up early one morning while my partner was still sleeping, looking over and feeling a sense of gratitude that I could experience this connection without the numbing effects of alcohol. I actually remembered our conversations from the night before, and I could be present for the small, tender moments that make up the base of a relationship.

When I reached my one-year sobriety milestone, our relationship was already well-established. That arbitrary line that I'd been warned not to cross before a year had long since been stepped over. But I was still in my version of sobriety, still committed to my recovery, still attending meetings and working with my sponsor. The relationship hadn't derailed my sobriety as the warnings suggested it might. But it definitely made things more complicated, adding all these emotional layers and things to think about that probably wouldn't have been there if I'd just focused on myself.

As time passed, our relationship deepened. We developed routines together, built shared memories, and began to envision a future that included marriage and children. I saw myself building a life with Lindsay, creating the family I'd always wanted.

I didn't just decide to propose on a whim. I was getting close to two years sober, had built a solid groundwork in my recovery, and genuinely felt ready for this step. So, I bought a ring, coordinated with family and friends to make sure they'd be there for the surprise, and planned out every detail so we could capture it all.

The day I was going to propose, I was a nervous wreck. I had so much to keep track of—keeping my mouth shut about the secret, making sure everyone would be there for the celebration afterward, and trying to handle my own emotions about taking such a huge step. In sobriety, you feel these big moments with an intensity that can be overwhelming. There's no chemical buffer, nothing to take the edge off the anxiety or dampen the emotions. You're present for every second.

When I got down on one knee and proposed, I was completely clear about the commitment I was making. The joy, the tears, the immediate "yes," I experienced it all with a clarity that allowed me to imprint every detail in my memory. The celebration afterward with our friends and family had the same quality of presence. I wasn't the guy in the corner doing shots or disappearing to the bathroom for a line. I was there, engaged, connecting.

Being engaged while sober presented its own unique challenges. Wedding planning is stressful for any couple, but doing it while maintaining my recovery practices requires additional mindfulness. There were industry events where alcohol flowed freely, vendor meetings at bars, and tastings that included wine pairings. I navigated these with the tools I'd developed, constantly aware of my boundaries and always prioritizing my sobriety.

What I discovered during this time was that commitment to sobriety has a different quality. It's not influenced by the moment's euphoria or temporarily lowered inhibitions. It's a choice made with full awareness, with all faculties intact. There's something powerful about that: knowing that my decision to commit was made with clarity, not in an altered state that might lead to morning-after regrets.

I've also learned that love in sobriety is both more challenging and more rewarding than relationships fueled by substances. More difficult because there's nowhere to hide from your own issues or the relationship's problems. More gratifying because the connections you form are authentic, based on who you really are rather than who alcohol or drugs make you appear to be.

Would I tell someone else to fall in love before hitting their one-year mark? Probably not. There's a reason everyone says to wait a year, and I've seen firsthand how messy it can get. But I don't regret it. That relationship was part of my recovery, and it taught me a lot about myself, about being intimate with someone, and about what I actually need and want in a partner.

I realized I have this tendency to throw my own well-being out the window just to keep the peace. Instead of being honest about what I need or setting boundaries, I just go along with whatever will avoid a fight. The relationship didn't create these patterns, but it definitely put a spotlight on them.

Recovery has taught me to be more thoughtful about all my relationships and how they fit into the life I'm building. I've learned that maintaining sobriety means being intentional about my environment and the people I surround myself with. As I continue growing, I'm discovering what feels supportive and sustainable for my journey.

Life doesn't always follow rulebooks, even ones that have helped millions achieve sobriety. Sometimes, hearts connect at inconvenient times. Sometimes, relationships form before we're fully ready. When that happens, the key is not rigid adherence to guidelines but rather a somewhat heightened awareness, increased support, and an unwavering commitment to sobriety above all else.

That's what I carry with me through this journey, from those first moments of connection through the engagement and wedding planning. My recovery remains my non-negotiable base, the ground on which I stand, regardless of what else is happening in my life.

Chapter 17

THE HARDEST PART ABOUT a public breakup isn't the breakup itself; it's everything that comes after. When two people in a normal relationship break up, they typically have the opportunity to process it privately. They can take time to heal, reflect, and move forward without scrutiny. But when you break up in the public eye, especially when you've canceled a wedding that was supposed to be just months away, you're suddenly thrust into a storm of speculation, accusations, and judgment.

I've experienced a lot in my life. I've lost my brother to addiction. I've fought my own battles with alcohol and cocaine. I've hit rock bottom and clawed my way back to recovery. However, the two months following the end of my engagement had been some of the most challenging of my life. Not because I regret the decision (I know it was the right one), but because of the narrative that has been created around it.

Let me be clear: ending an engagement is never easy, especially when you care deeply about the person you're with. There were signs we weren't right for each other, even though we both worked hard in ten months of couples therapy. She showed up for me in meaningful ways, and I'll always value the love and commitment she brought to our relationship. But the same conflicts kept resurfacing, and we couldn't find a way through them. But when I looked ahead to the wedding that was fast approaching, I couldn't ignore my gut feeling that this wasn't right for either of us.

What was most difficult was how quickly the narrative spun out of my control. Within days, stories were circulating that painted me as the villain: as someone who strung along their partner only to brutally dump them at the last minute. The truth was way messier and more painful for both of us. We'd been having the same fights over and over for months, falling into the same toxic patterns, trying everything we could think of to fix what was broken between us. But relationships aren't like broken bones; sometimes you can't just set them and wait for them to heal.

Then came the accusations about my recovery. This cut deeper than anything else. Sobriety isn't just something I do; it's who I am. It's the foundation upon which I've built my new life. To have that questioned, to have people insinuate I'd been drinking or using again, felt like someone attacking the core of my identity.

The truth about my sobriety is simple but often misunderstood. I'm clean from alcohol and cocaine, the substances that nearly killed me. I do use THC occasionally to manage anxiety, depression, and PTSD. Some people call this "California sober," though I've never hidden this aspect of my recovery. I've been open about it since Season Five.

I use THC as a harm reduction alternative to prescription medications like Xanax or Ambien. I have a small vape pen that I might use at night or in the afternoon if I need to take the edge off anxiety. It doesn't lead me to drink. It doesn't make me want cocaine. It just helps me manage my mental health in a way that works for me.

For people who don't understand addiction, this nuance can be confusing. They think sobriety is all or nothing. But recovery is personal. My therapist supports my approach. My sponsor understands it. The people who actually care about my well-being see that I'm healthier and more stable than I've been in years.

Still, the accusations persisted. I'd read articles claiming I was drunk at airports. People would analyze photos of me, claiming my eyes looked glazed or my behavior seemed off. One day, I made the mistake of looking at social media comments. "He's clearly using again," someone wrote with absolute certainty, despite never having met me.

The paparazzi started camping outside my apartment. One morning, I had to leave for a meeting, and the second I walked outside, cameras started going off everywhere. I wasn't ready for that shit. I was just trying to make it through the day, trying to deal with the anxiety and pain of everything falling apart, and now these people were documenting every look on my face and picking it apart. "Carl looking somber," the caption would read as if that was surprising for someone going through a breakup.

I hid out at a friend's place and, for a while, I didn't go outside. It wasn't just the paparazzi; it was the fear of running into someone who had read these stories and formed an opinion about me based on half-truths and speculation. Would they confront me? Would they say something hurtful? Would they look at me with judgment or pity? The anxiety was paralyzing.

And while I was trying to wrap my head around all this, I still had to deal with the actual logistics of canceling a wedding. I ended up paying over $100,000 out of my own pocket for all the cancellation fees. I didn't want our guests getting screwed over with charges they couldn't get back. I sent an email providing everyone with a specific timeframe to cancel and receive a full refund. Yet somehow, stories circulated that I was stiffing our wedding guests with the bill. It was the opposite of the truth, but it became part of the narrative anyway.

There were days during this period when I questioned whether I wanted to be on this earth anymore. That's not easy to admit, but it's the truth. When you wake up day after day to see your name in the news next to words like lies and manipulation, when something as sacred as your sobriety is being questioned, when you feel like you can't escape the noise and find a moment of peace, it takes a toll.

What made it even harder was having to re-explain myself to friends and family repeatedly. The people closest to me weren't questioning my sobriety, but they were concerned about the toll all this was taking on me. I had to relive the details of the breakup, explain my side of the story, and reassure them I was okay, all while I was still processing everything myself.

People seemed to forget that I'm a human being who has been through significant trauma. I've lost my brother. I nearly lost myself to addiction. I've spent the last four years rebuilding my life, one day at a time. I'm not perfect; far from it. But I'm trying. Every day, I wake up and choose sobriety. I choose to face life on life's terms, without escape mechanisms. I choose to be honest, even when it's difficult. I choose to take responsibility for my actions, even when it would be easier to blame others.

The hardest part was feeling misunderstood. Ending the relationship was painful because I cared deeply about her, and I knew she cared for me. But despite that love, our dynamic wasn't healthy, and walking away, as hard as it was, felt like the most compassionate choice for both of us. The pattern of conflict, the lack of trust, the communication breakdowns: they weren't getting better, despite our efforts in couples therapy. I had to be honest with myself: if we went forward, the conflicts we couldn't resolve now would likely follow us into marriage. I wanted a future built on stability and trust, and despite the love we had, I couldn't see us creating that together. I couldn't go through with the wedding knowing what I knew.

I believe in the sanctity of marriage. It should be a celebration of a relationship, not a Band-Aid for a broken one. Walking away from the engagement was one of the hardest decisions I've ever made, but I stand by it. Every weekend, thousands of couples get married, knowing it's not the right thing to do. They go through with it anyway, have kids, buy houses, and end up divorced within a few years. I didn't want that for either of us.

In the middle of all this mayhem, I decided to move to Brooklyn. I needed a fresh start somewhere I wouldn't be constantly thinking about the relationship and where I wouldn't bump into fans every time I left my apartment. The place I'd been living wasn't good for me: the rent was ridiculous, and I couldn't walk down the street without someone recognizing me. It was an ego stroke at times, sure, but it was also incredibly draining, especially when I was trying to heal.

Brooklyn has been a breath of fresh air. It's more relaxed, more diverse, has more to do, and more space to breathe. I can go for runs along the water. I can sit in coffee shops without being approached for photos. I'm still recognized occasionally, but the vibe is different. People are more chill and real here. During my first week, this couple came up to me, told me they supported me, and welcomed me to the neighborhood. They didn't ask for a selfie or try to dig into my business. It was just a quick thing, but it meant everything to me when I was going through such a rough time.

Slowly, I've been rebuilding my base. I got a new apartment. I bought furniture. I established new routines. Every day, I wake up and take my thyroid medication (I have hypothyroidism and have been taking levothyroxine for fifteen years). I turn on my meditation app and do a ten-minute guided meditation while getting ready. I eat a granola bar and log onto Zoom for my daily AA meeting from eight to nine a.m. It's a simple routine, but it grounds me.

The further I get from the old environment and the toxic dynamics, the better I feel. I'm still processing the breakup and the public fallout, but I'm doing it on my own terms, in my own space. I'm focusing on my sobriety, my mental health, and my personal growth. I'm taking things one day at a time, as we say in recovery.

I'm also trying to take the high road. Despite everything, I haven't disparaged my ex in the media. I haven't gone on podcasts to tell "my side" of the story. I haven't done any press that wasn't approved. I've tried to maintain my dignity and integrity through all of this, even when it would have been easier to lash out in response to the accusations being made about me.

What I've learned from all this is that what people think they know about you isn't real. People see little pieces of information, clips from TV shows, stuff on social media, and they think they have the full picture. They're making judgments about someone they've never even met based on stories that are written to get clicks and views.

But I know who I am. I know what I've been through. I know why I made the choices I made. And at the end of the day, that's what matters.

Looking ahead, I'm just trying to focus on growing and healing. I've learned a ton about myself from this relationship and how it ended. I've seen my codependent issues, how I communicate (or don't), and my boundaries, which apparently I don't have enough of. I've learned about what I need in a partner and what dynamics don't work for me. I've gained a clearer understanding of how my past trauma affects my present relationships.

I hope one day, people will understand that ending the engagement was an act of courage, not cruelty. It would have been easier to go through with the wedding to avoid public scrutiny and judgment. But it wouldn't have been right for either of us. Sometimes, the hardest decisions are also the most compassionate ones.

In the meantime, I'll continue to focus on my sobriety, one day at a time. I'll continue to speak my truth, even when it's misunderstood. I'll continue to live with integrity, even when it would be easier not to. And I'll continue to believe that with time, the truth always reveals itself.

Right now, I'm finding peace in the simple stuff: my morning meditation, running along the water, talking with friends who actually know me, and just having quiet time alone in my new place. I'm rebuilding bit by bit, grateful for what I've learned even though some of it hurt like hell, and I'm hopeful about whatever comes next.

The public fallout has been one of the most challenging experiences of my life, but like everything else I've been through, it's teaching me resilience, patience, and self-compassion. It's reinforcing what I already knew: that external validation is fleeting, but inner peace and authenticity are what truly matter.

I don't know what the future holds. Even though the season of our breakup and the subsequent summer after that have aired, there are still different views. I don't know if people will eventually see the bigger picture or if some will remain committed to seeing me as the bad guy. What I do know is that I can't control any of that. I can only control my actions, my responses, and my commitment to living soberly and authentically.

And that's enough. It has to be.

Chapter 18

As I SIT HERE reflecting on the path that's brought me to this point, I can't help but marvel at life's unpredictable turns. If someone had told me four years ago, when I was still in the throes of addiction, blacking out regularly, doing lines in bathroom stalls, and waking up filled with regret, that I'd one day be opening a non-alcoholic bar in Brooklyn, I would have laughed in their face. Yet here I am, in 2024, watching Soft Bar + Café come to life, with opening day set for September 2025. Life has a funny way of turning your worst moments into the thing you're meant to do.

Getting from rock bottom to where I am now hasn't been a straight line. There've been wrong turns, dead ends, and times when I almost said screw it and gave up. But that's recovery for you. It's not like you arrive somewhere and you're done. It's something you do every single day, sometimes crawling, sometimes running, but always trying to keep moving forward.

When I got sober in January 2021, I had no grand vision for my future. I just wanted to survive. I wanted to wake up without a hangover. I wanted to remember the night before. I wanted to look in the mirror and not hate the person staring back at me. My goals were small because they had to be. In early sobriety, you learn to celebrate the most minor victories—making your bed in the morning, showing up to work on time, and having an honest conversation without the need for liquid courage.

I couldn't have known then how recovery would reshape every aspect of my life, from my relationships to my career to my sense of purpose. I couldn't have anticipated how it would strip away the layers of false confidence and bravado, forcing me to confront the honest Carl underneath—a Carl who was deeply insecure, struggled with self-worth and used substances to numb the pain of not feeling good enough.

That's the thing about recovery—it's not just about stopping drinking or using. It's about addressing the reasons you started in the first place. It's about healing wounds you didn't even know you had. It's about learning to live authentically in a world that often encourages the opposite.

For me, recovery meant reckoning with the trauma of losing my brother to addiction. It meant addressing the complicated relationship with my father, who had his own struggles. It meant finally admitting the stuff I'd been doing wrong—always needing people to tell me I was good enough, being terrified of getting rejected, and putting everyone else's needs before my own. It meant figuring out how to feel good about myself without needing to achieve something or get praise or have everyone like me.

This inner work isn't glamorous. It doesn't make for compelling television. But it's the most critical work I've ever done. Without it, I might have stopped drinking, but I wouldn't have truly changed. And I certainly wouldn't be where I am today, on the cusp of opening a business that represents everything I've learned and everything I believe in.

Soft Bar + Café isn't just some business idea for me. It's basically my whole recovery story in one place. When I got sober, one of the hardest things was trying to hang out anywhere without feeling completely out of place. No matter where I went, I felt like I didn't belong. I'd order a club soda with lime, then watch everyone else enjoy craft cocktails or fine wines, feeling like I was getting the short end of the stick simply because I chose not to drink.

I started to realize that this was a gap in the market, but more importantly, it was a gap in our culture. Why should people who don't drink alcohol—whether for recovery reasons, health reasons, or personal preference—have a lesser experience when they go out? Why should non-alcoholic options be an afterthought, a joke, something restaurants and bars reluctantly provide rather than proudly feature?

The idea for Soft Bar + Café came from these questions. I wanted to create a space where everyone could enjoy the social aspects of bar culture without the pressure to drink. A place with the ambiance, the craftsmanship, and the attention to detail you'd find in a high-end cocktail bar, but with beverages explicitly designed to be consumed without alcohol.

This isn't a "sober bar." I'm careful about that distinction. It's a bar for everyone—for those in recovery, yes, but also for pregnant women who want to go out with friends, for health-conscious individuals who don't want a hangover the next day, for the sober-curious who are taking a break from drinking but still want to socialize, and even for drinkers who simply want a night off.

I've been intentional about every aspect of Soft Bar, from the language we use (you won't see the word "mocktails" anywhere) to the ingredients we source. We're collaborating with Rich Millwater, formerly of Eleven Madison Park, to craft "soft cocktails" that stand on their own merit, not as lesser versions of alcoholic beverages. We're collaborating with Dr. Brooke Scheller, an expert in sober nutrition, to incorporate functional ingredients that not only taste good but also provide benefits for the mind and body.

Even our coffee program, led by Antonia Petaccio, is carefully designed. Coffee is our Trojan horse—a familiar entry point for people who might be hesitant to try a non-alcoholic bar. Once they walk in, they'll see all these options they probably never thought about.

Getting to this point has been tough as hell. Finding investors, hunting for the right location, dealing with all the bureaucracy of opening a business in New York City—none of it has been easy. But compared to getting into recovery, compared to facing my demons and rebuilding my life from the ground up, these obstacles have felt manageable.

What has been most rewarding is the response I've received from friends, the sober community, and people who simply recognize the need for more inclusive social spaces. Every time we host a pop-up event with our Sprinter van, I see the excitement in people's eyes when they taste a non-alcoholic beverage that has been crafted with the same care and creativity as any cocktail. I hear their stories—about recovery, pregnancy, health journeys, and simply wanting options beyond sugary sodas or bland sparkling water.

These moments remind me why I'm doing this. They remind me that my pain—the struggles with addiction, the rock bottom moments, the hard work of recovery—can be transformed into something that helps others. That's the beauty of this journey. What once nearly destroyed me has become the basis for something that might make a difference in people's lives.

Of course, Soft Bar isn't the only way I'm channeling my recovery into purpose. I've also rejoined Loverboy to help develop their non-alcoholic line. It's a full-circle moment that I never could have predicted. When I was drinking, working at an alcohol company made sense—it aligned with my lifestyle, gave me easy access to the substance I craved, and allowed me to blend my partying with my professional life in a way that seemed convenient but was ultimately destructive.

Leaving Loverboy was necessary for my early recovery. I couldn't be around alcohol all the time and couldn't attend events where drinking was the main activity. But time brings clarity and healing. Working with Kyle on the non-alcoholic line feels right in a way I couldn't have imagined when I first entered recovery. It's a chance to bring my experience, perspective, and passion for non-alcoholic options to a well-established brand, reaching people who might never have set foot in Soft Bar.

The fact that Kyle was open to this collaboration and saw the value in expanding into the non-alcoholic space speaks to the strength of our friendship despite the professional tensions we've experienced. It would have been easy for him to move forward without me, to develop non-alcoholic products on his own. But he recognized what I could bring to the table—not just my reality TV platform, but my lived experience with sobriety and my understanding of what people in recovery are looking for.

This is the power of authentic relationships. They weather storms. They adapt and evolve. They find new expressions that honor the past while creating space for growth. My friendship with Kyle has changed over the years, as all relationships do, but its foundation remains solid.

The same can't be said for all the relationships in my life. Recovery has a way of clarifying which connections are based on substance and which ones have substance. Some friendships naturally faded as my lifestyle changed. Others grew stronger as I showed up more authentically, more consistently, and more present. New relationships formed with people who knew me only as recovery Carl, who never experienced the chaos of my drinking days.

And then there are the romantic relationships. Dating in recovery has been one of the most challenging aspects of this journey, especially in the early days. Adding the intensity of romantic love to that mix can be destabilizing.

But life doesn't always follow rulebooks. Sometimes, feelings develop before you're fully ready for them. And learning to navigate those waters without alcohol—without the liquid courage for first dates, without the chemical buffer for conflicts, without the numbing effect of heartbreak—has been a crash course in emotional maturity.

What I've discovered is that love in recovery has a clarity that was missing in my drinking days. I'm more attuned to red flags, more aware of my patterns, and more honest about my needs and boundaries. I'm less likely to stay in situations that don't serve me simply because they're familiar or provide temporary comfort. I'm more capable of showing up fully, of being present through the highs and lows, of navigating conflicts without avoidance or eruption.

That's not to say I've mastered it, far from it. I still screw up. I still fall into those codependent habits sometimes. I still have moments where my old insecurities come back, where stuff from my past messes with what's happening now. But the difference is that I can see it happening. I can recognize them, name them, and work through them with the help of my sponsor, my therapist, and my support network.

This awareness extends beyond romantic relationships to all areas of my life. I'm more intentional about the work I take on, the people I surround myself with and the environments I place myself in. I'm more protective of my energy, more mindful of my triggers, and more committed to maintaining the practices that support my recovery.

Moving to Brooklyn was part of trying to be more intentional about my life. I needed a fresh start, somewhere that wasn't loaded with memories, a place where I could just be a regular person instead of getting recognized every time I walked outside. The move has given me room to breathe, to reflect, to rebuild. It's given me a physical distance that mirrors the emotional distance I needed to establish from patterns and dynamics that no longer served me.

The public scrutiny of my relationships, the speculation about my recovery, the narrative that often paints me as the bad guy despite my best efforts—these challenges have tested my resolve, pushed me to dig deeper into my recovery tools, and forced me to practice the principles of AA in all my affairs, not just when it's convenient.

I won't pretend it's been easy. There have been days when I questioned whether the public eye was the right place for me and whether the benefits of my platform outweighed the costs to my mental health. There have been moments when I longed for anonymity, for the ability to make mistakes without millions of viewers analyzing every decision, every expression, every word.

But then I remember the messages I receive from people who have been inspired by my recovery journey and who have found hope in seeing someone navigate this path while maintaining a public life. I remember the conversations I've had at events where someone quietly pulls me aside to share their own struggles with substances, their own fears about getting sober, and their own questions about what life looks like on the other side of addiction.

These moments remind me that visibility matters. Representation matters. Seeing someone you can relate to walk a path you're considering can make all the difference. If my story helps even one person take that first step toward recovery, then the challenges of being public about this journey are worth it.

And now, with Soft Bar + Café, I have the opportunity to create a physical space where people can experience the benefits of mindful consumption, where they can socialize without substances, where they can feel included rather than bothered for their choice not to drink. It's a tangible extension of the work I've been doing through my platform, a way to reach people who might never watch *Summer House* but who still seek connection, community, and a sense of belonging.

I'm under no illusion that this journey is complete. Recovery is ongoing. Personal growth is continuing. The work of addressing past trauma, developing healthy coping mechanisms, and building authentic relationships never really ends. There will be new challenges, new insights, and new growth opportunities. There will be days when I struggle, when old patterns resurface, when the weight of it all feels overwhelming.

But I'm equipped now in a way I wasn't before. I have tools. I have support. I have clarity about who I am and what matters to me. I know my worth now, and it doesn't come from what other people think of me. I have something I'm working toward that matters more than whether people like me or not.

Most importantly, I have perspective. I know what it's like to hit rock bottom. I see the desperation of addiction, the emptiness of waking up with yet another hangover, and the shame of not remembering what you said or did the night before. I know the pain of watching someone you love lose their battle with substances, the grief that comes with recognizing your own powerlessness over their choices, and the fear that you might follow the same path.

This perspective is invaluable. It keeps me grateful for where I am now, even when things get tough. It reminds me that the worst day sober is still better than the best day I had when I was drinking. It keeps me grounded when success comes my way, humble when opportunities present themselves, and mindful of the fact that everything I have built could be lost if I were to return to old patterns.

As I look ahead to the opening of Soft Bar + Café, to the continued development of non-alcoholic Loverboy, and to whatever the future holds for my personal and professional life, I carry this perspective with me. I approach each new venture, each new relationship, each new day with the awareness that recovery is the groundwork upon which everything else stands. Without it, nothing else is possible. With it, the possibilities are endless.

This isn't the end of my story, not even close. It's a moment to stop and take stock of where I've been and where I'm heading next. There's still so much more

I want to share, so many more lessons I need to learn and figure out. Before I keep moving forward, I want to acknowledge everything that's happened on this journey that brought me to this point.

Chapter 19

I'M STANDING IN THE middle of my friend's front yard in New Jersey on the Soft Bar Friends and Family soft launch night, August 1, 2024, overwhelmed by the energy in the open air. The outdoor space is packed. Friends, family, cast members, industry folks, and curious supporters mingle, sipping expertly crafted non-alcoholic beverages we brought to preview Soft Bar + Café. My mom is here, beaming with pride.

This moment feels surreal. Three years ago, I was hitting rock bottom, wondering if I'd ever find purpose again. Now, I'm watching as Rich, our head mixologist, crafts intricate soft cocktails at the pop-up bar we set up on the patio. I overhear conversations from guests expressing surprise at how complex and satisfying the drinks are without alcohol. The portable coffee station is buzzing with activity as Antonia serves our specialty coffee from carafes. The air is filled with genuine connection and conversation, exactly what I envisioned for this space.

I catch my mom's eye from across the yard. She's talking with some of my friends who've known me since Pittsburgh, people who saw me at my worst. The look on her face says everything: relief, joy, and that proud mom look that reminds me how far I've actually come. My mom has been through it all with me: the late-night calls when I was drunk and spiraling, the worried visits when she knew something was wrong but I wouldn't admit it, and the tearful conversations after my brother passed away. She deserves this moment as much as I do.

Opening Soft Bar has been more than just launching a business. It has been a transformative experience. It's been about creating a real, physical space that represents my recovery: somewhere that showcases everything I've learned about connecting with people, being genuine, and living intentionally. Every detail, from the lighting to how we set up the seating to where we get our ingredients, all of it comes from what I believe in now.

The road to this moment wasn't smooth. There were financing challenges, supply chain issues, and construction delays. All the typical headaches of launching a brick-and-mortar business in New York City. There were moments when I questioned whether I was in over my head and whether I had the business acumen to pull this off. But my recovery has taught me resilience. It has taught me to face challenges directly rather than escape from them. It has taught me to ask for help when I need it and to trust the process, even when the outcome isn't guaranteed.

I've been particularly moved by the way the recovery community has embraced the concept of Soft Bar. In the weeks leading up to our soft launch, I received numerous messages from people in recovery who were desperate to have a place where they could socialize and feel included without feeling completely left out. One message that really resonated with me came from a woman who had just celebrated her one-year mark in recovery. She wrote that seeing someone like me (someone in the public eye who was open about his struggles and his healing) gave her hope that she could rebuild her life, too.

That's what drives me: the possibility that my story might help someone else find their way out of addiction. It's why I agreed to film Season Nine of *Summer House* despite the challenges of having my personal life on display. It's why I'm launching a podcast focused on recovery and wellness. And it's why I poured my heart into writing this book.

The book process was more intense than I ever imagined. Revisiting the darkest periods of my life—the rock bottom moments, the pain I caused others, the self-hatred that fueled my addiction—was excruciating at times. There were days when I had to step away from the writing when the memories became too overwhelming. But there was healing in the telling, too. Articulating my experiences forced me to make sense of them, to find meaning in suffering, and to recognize the growth that came from my lowest points.

I didn't write this book to be inspirational in some superficial, Instagram-quote kind of way. I wrote it, to be honest. Brutally, uncomfortably honest. I wanted to strip away the glamor that our culture often associates with drinking and drug use. I wanted to show the gritty reality of addiction, the day-to-day degradation of the spirit, and the slow erosion of self-worth. I wanted readers to understand that recovery isn't about willpower or discipline but about connection, community, and finding purpose beyond the next drink or the next high.

At the same time, I wanted to offer hope. Not the false hope that recovery is easy or that one day you wake up, and all the urges are gone. But the real hope that comes from knowing others have walked this path before you is that they've faced the same demons and found a way through. The hope that comes from seeing concrete examples of lives rebuilt, of joy rediscovered, of purpose reclaimed.

If even one person reads this book and recognizes their own story in mine, if they see that recovery is possible even from the most bottomless pit of addiction, if they take that first step toward healing because something I shared resonated with them, then every painful memory revisited, every vulnerability exposed, will have been worth it.

Since I began my recovery in January 2021, I've been on a journey of continuous discovery. I've learned what Carl looks like without substances to numb his insecurities or amplify his confidence. I've learned what Carl sounds like when he's speaking from a place of authenticity rather than performance. I've learned what Carl values when he's not chasing external validation or temporary escape.

This self-discovery continues with each new venture, each new relationship, and each new challenge. Filming Season Nine of *Summer House* as a person in recovery in a house full of alcohol was yet another learning experience. It forced me to develop new social muscles, find ways to connect with people whose lifestyles differ from mine, and set boundaries without isolating myself.

The podcast is the next frontier. I'm excited to have deeper conversations about recovery, mental health, and personal growth than the time limits of reality TV typically allow for. I want to interview experts in addiction medicine, people with long-term recovery, and family members affected by a loved one's substance use.

Anyone who can help people understand what addiction truly is and what it takes to overcome it.

Outside of all these projects I'm working on, I'm really excited about how people are starting to think differently about drinking and drugs. More people are questioning their relationship with drinking, exploring sober curiosity, and seeking alternatives to the traditional alcohol-centered social scene. Non-alcoholic beverage sales are surging. "Dry January" and "Sober October" have become mainstream terms. Celebrities and influencers are opening up about their decisions to cut back or quit drinking entirely.

I'm not naive enough to think that alcohol will ever stop being a central feature of American social life. However, I do believe we're experiencing a shift toward more mindful consumption, one that involves questioning rather than automatically accepting drinking culture and creating space for those who choose not to participate in it.

Soft Bar is my contribution to this movement. It's a real place that represents everything I believe in now that I'm sober: being authentic, connecting with others, staying present, and taking care of myself. It's proof that just because you don't drink doesn't mean you have to be isolated or bored out of your mind. It's a business, obviously, but it's also something I really believe in. To normalize non-drinking, to elevate non-alcoholic options beyond an afterthought, and to create inclusive spaces where everyone feels welcome regardless of their relationship with substances.

As I look around the backyard on this soft launch night, I feel a deep sense of gratitude. Gratitude for the team that helped bring Soft Bar to life: Brian, Cristopher, Angela, Rich, Dr. Brooke, Antonia, Rachel, Abby and countless others who believed in the vision. Gratitude for my family and friends who supported me through the darkest days of my addiction and the challenging early days of recovery. Gratitude to the viewers and readers who have followed my journey, who have shared their own stories, and who have made me feel less alone in this very public process of healing.

Most of all, I'm grateful for the gift of clarity. Recovery has given me the ability to be present for moments like this. I can feel everything now without needing to numb it or run away from it. I can actually connect with people for real instead of putting on some act. I can work on things that matter to me instead of just looking for ways to escape.

This clarity extends to my vision for the future. I hope to expand Soft Bar beyond Brooklyn, bringing this concept to other cities where people in recovery or those seeking alternatives to the drinking culture might benefit from it. I plan to continue using my platform, reality TV, the podcast, this book, to destigmatize addiction and recovery, to encourage open conversation about mental health, and to show that vulnerability is not weakness but courage.

I hope to continue growing personally, to keep addressing the underlying issues that contributed to my addiction, and to build relationships based on authenticity rather than convenience or performance. I hope to be a source of support for others on their recovery journeys and to give back some of what was given to me when I needed it most.

None of this is guaranteed, of course. Recovery is a daily choice, a continuous process of growth and transformation. There will be challenges ahead, both personal and professional, as well as emotional. There will be moments of doubt, of struggle, of wishing for the easy escape that substances once provided. There will be days when the weight of past mistakes feels overwhelming and when the work of rebuilding seems insurmountable.

But I face these possibilities with a foundation I never had before. I have tools for managing difficult emotions without substances. I have a community of support that understands the unique challenges of recovery. I have gained a deeper understanding of myself, including my triggers, patterns, values, and self-worth. I have a purpose beyond the next party, the next drink, the next high.

Standing here in my friend's New Jersey front yard on this Friends and Family soft launch night, surrounded by people who represent different chapters of my life, from childhood friends to *Summer House* cast members to recovery peers, I'm struck by the continuity amid the change. I'm still Carl from Pittsburgh with the same insecurities, the same desire for connection, the same need for meaning and purpose. But I'm also a new version of that Carl: one who faces life directly rather than escaping it, who builds rather than destroys, who shows up authentically rather than performing.

This duality is what recovery is all about: honoring who you've been while becoming who you're meant to be, acknowledging your mistakes while refusing to be defined by them, and carrying your past with you while not allowing it to determine your future.

As I prepare to address the crowd gathered in the garden to thank them for being part of this milestone, I reflect on the message I want to convey to them. And by extension, what message I want to leave the readers of this book with. It's something my sponsor told me in early recovery when I was struggling to imagine a life without substances, when I was questioning whether the pain of change was worth it.

He said, "Recovery isn't about what you give up. It's about what you gain."

In the nearly five years since I started my recovery journey, I've gained more than I ever imagined possible. I've gained genuine connections with people who know the real me, not just the party persona. I've gained clarity about my values and purpose. I've gained self-respect and the respect of others. I've gained the ability to be present for both joy and pain without numbing or escaping. I've gained businesses and ventures that align with who I really am rather than who I pretend to be. I've gained the trust of friends and family who once worried about what version of Carl they'd encounter on any given day.

Most importantly, I've gained the knowledge that I am not my addiction. I am not my mistakes. I am not defined by my worst moments. I am a person in progress, with flaws and strengths, with a past that shapes me but doesn't define me, with a future that's unwritten but full of possibility.

And so are you.

Whether you're reading this book because you're struggling with substances yourself, because you love someone who is, or simply because you're curious about my journey, I want you to know this: change is possible. Healing is possible. A life beyond your current pain is possible.

It won't be easy. It won't be linear. It will require courage, honesty, vulnerability, and a supportive environment. It will mean facing truths about yourself that you've spent years avoiding. It will mean developing new ways of coping with emotions you've been numbing. It will mean redefining your relationship with yourself and others.

But on the other side of that work is a life of presence, of authenticity, of purpose. A life where you no longer need to escape because reality, even with its challenges and pain, is worth experiencing fully. A life where connections are genuine, where accomplishments are meaningful, where joy is unfiltered.

That's what I've found in recovery. That's what I want to keep building as I move forward with Soft Bar, with the podcast, and with whatever ventures and relationships the future holds. That's what I wish for everyone who reads these words.

The journey continues, one day at a time. And I'm grateful for each step.

Acknowledgments

To my family: This comes first because you've been there from the beginning. Mom, you never gave up on me, even when I gave you every reason to. You've been my rock through the absolute worst times of my life. Seeing you and Dad stand on that lawn after Curtis died, seeing you at the Soft Bar launch, those moments remind me why I keep fighting to be better. I love you. Lou, thank you for loving my mom and being a steady presence in our family. Dad, thank you for always showing up when it mattered most and for teaching me what it means to work hard and keep pushing forward. I'm proud to call you my Dad and thank you for allowing me grace to be so open publicly about my life. I'm grateful for everything you've done for me and for the relationship we have today. Love you pops!

To my Summer House family: Thank you for allowing me to be me, even when that meant being a complete mess. A lot of you knew the real me from day 1 but only saw glimpses of that on weekends. You've watched me at my worst and celebrated with me at my best. Kyle and Amanda, you two have been there through everything: the dark days, the breakthrough moments, all of it. To the rest of the cast Lindsay, Danielle, Paige, Ciara, Andrea, West, Jesse thank you for the memories, the car rides, the laughs, and for being there for me.

To the Summer House producers and the entire Bravo team: Thank you for seeing me as a person first, especially during the hardest moments of my life. You gave me space to heal and supported my decision to get sober, even when it complicated filming. You never pressured me to turn my grief into content. You gave me space to heal and supported my decision to get sober, even when it complicated filming. That humanity meant everything to me. Thank you for trusting me to tell my story honestly.

To my friends who stuck with me through everything: You know who you are. Cake eaters from Upper St Clair, and many friends from Pittsburgh, Syracuse, Los Angeles and some met me in New York, and some came into my life through the show. Thank you for not giving up on me when I was impossible to be around. Thank you for the honest conversations, for calling me out when I needed it, and for celebrating my goals and milestones like they were your own.

Kyle and Amanda, I'm mentioning you again because you deserve it. And Nick, Emily, Dylan, and the entire Loverboy team, thank you for understanding when I needed to step back and thank you for welcoming me back in a way that supported my recovery. That meant more than you know. Good times, no regrets.

To the Soft Bar team: Brian, Cristopher, Angela, HERE, WE ARE. There's too many people to name that have inspired this vision and concept but I hope the saying rains true, a rising tide lifts all boats. Thank you for believing in this vision, thank you for helping me build something that actually matters. You transformed an idea born from my own struggle into a tangible space where people can connect and feel included. That means everything to me.

To Rising Action Publishing, specifically Alex Brown and Tina Beier: Thank you for believing in me before I even thought this was possible. I wanted to help people and you helped me find my voice on the page and pushed me to go deeper, to be more honest, even when it hurt. You helped me turn years of pain and growth into something that might actually help someone else. Ashley Detweiler, Abby Sharp, and Soffia Ponson, thank you for your work on the marketing side and for believing this story deserved to reach people.

To the Audible team: Hillary Doyle, Lauren Kuefner, Caitlyn Livingston, Sacco, Anthony Casella, Billy Hall, Brandt Hale, Amil Dave, and Dipti Kapadia, thank you for bringing this story to life in audio form. Telling my story out loud, in my own voice, felt important and real. Thank you for making that possible and for caring about getting it right.

Miss Nat Mack, thank you for designing a cover that effectively captures the essence of this book.

Daniel Rahal, thank you for capturing the perfect photos for the cover. Nikki Siminson, Jesus Peral and Haley Wilkinson, thank you all for making me presentable in the photos.

Thank you to Angie Ankier and the MR PORTER team for the clothes for the cover shoot.

To the fans who've followed my journey: Thank you for sticking with me through the messy parts, for the messages of support when I needed them most, and for showing up to Soft Bar and believing in what we're building. Your encouragement has meant more than you know.

And finally, to anyone reading this who's struggling with addiction or loving someone who is: Thank you for giving my story a chance. I hope it helps. That's why I wrote it.

Carl